The Ugly Chinaman

Bo Yang was born in China in 1920 and fled to Taiwan in 1949 on the eve of the communist takeover. A poet, novelist, essayist and historian, Bo Yang was jailed for ten years for translating into Chinese a Popeye cartoon that the Taiwan authorities found offensive. Upon his release in 1977, he began to give the speeches on the Ugly Chinaman phenomenon that form the core of this book. Bo Yang lives in Taipei with his wife, the poet Chang Hsiang-hua.

Don J. Cohn studied Chinese at Oberlin College and Columbia University has lived in China, Hong Kong and Taiwan for over a decade. He is books editor of *Far Eastern Economic Review* in Hong Kong, where he writes frequently on travel and the arts. Jing Qing grew up in Beijing and has lived in Oslo and Auckland. She has translated Clive Bell's *Civilisation* and Rupert Wilkinson's *The Prefect* into Chinese. Jing Qing and Don Cohn live in Hong Kong with their daughter Libbie Momo.

The Ugly Chinaman
and the crisis of Chinese culture

Bo Yang

Translated and edited by
Don J. Cohn and Jing Qing

ALLEN & UNWIN

The translation of '"The Ugly Chinaman"'—a speech given at Iowa
University', is based on a version that appeared in *Renditions: A
Chinese English Translation Magazine,* No. 23, Spring 1985, published
by the Chinese University of Hong Kong.

First published 1992
Third impression 1992
Allen & Unwin Pty Ltd
9 Atchison Street, St. Leonards, NSW 2065

National Library of Australia
Cataloguing-in-Publication entry:

Yang, Bo, 1920– .
The Ugly Chinaman and the crisis of Chinese culture.

ISBN 1 86373 116 4.

1. China—Civilization. 2. China—Social life and customs.
I. Cohn, Don. II. Qing, Jing. III. Title.

951

Set in 10/11.5 pt Times by DOCUPRO, Sydney
Printed by SRM Production Services Sdn Bhd, Malaysia

Contents

Preface to the English translation

The road taken by the Chinese writer is a treacherous one, full of twists and turns. I have been making my living as a writer for over 40 years. I began in the 1950s by writing fiction. In the 1960s, I wrote a number of newspaper columns in which I criticised various inequalities and injustices in Taiwan society. Because of what I wrote, the Kuomintang Government accused me of being a 'communist spy', jailed me, and attempted to get a military tribunal to sentence me to death. Eventually my sentence was reduced to twelve years in prison. My long stint behind bars gave me time to think about China's problems, and to confirm the basic premise of everything I had written before: 'Every problem in contemporary Chinese society originates in the traditional culture of the soy paste vat'.

When I was released from prison in the late 1970s, I had planned to write a book based on this premise in order to shake the Chinese people out of their muddleheaded complacency and arrogance, but at the time I was working on my *Outline History of the Chinese People*, and editing a series of books on Chinese history that I had begun writing in prison, so I put the idea on the back burner.

In 1984, when I was taking part in an international writers' conference at Iowa University in the USA, a Chinese student association invited me to address them. Suddenly all the thoughts stored up inside me—those ideas I had wanted to shape into a book, but which I was not allowed to talk about in public (as a condition for my release from prison)—surged into my consciousness like a tidal wave. So I decided to use that occasion to talk about this long-suppressed topic. I entitled my talk 'The Ugly Chinaman'* because I wanted to shock my compatriots into self-understanding.

---

* This archaic and derogatory term, bound to offend some readers, is deliberately used throughout this translation with Bo Yang's approval. (Translators)

Not long after this, an anthology of articles about the Ugly Chinaman by myself and others (including the talk I gave at Iowa University), originally published in Chinese in Taiwan, was translated into Japanese and Korean, and in 1986 five different Chinese editions were published in mainland China. This set off what the media in China referred to as 'Bo Yang fever'. Within one year, however, the Beijing *Guangming Daily*, the Chinese Communist Party's leading newspaper for intellectuals, published a long critical attack on the book (see 'Are Chinamen so ugly?' by Sun Guodong, p. 101). This in turn provoked a nationwide anti-Bo Yang campaign in China that was reminiscent of the harrowing 'struggle' sessions common during the Cultural Revolution. Later, I learned from the newspapers that my book *The Ugly Chinaman* had been a pawn in a power struggle taking place in the higher echelons of the Party. Hu Yaobang, then communist party secretary, had recommended the book to his subordinates. This was just the sort of lame excuse the conservative faction was looking for, and they attacked the book as a way of harassing Hu Yaobang. The fierceness of the accusations made me feel grateful for the fact that I do not live in mainland China, but rather in relatively liberal and democratic Taiwan.

In 1988 I went back to China for the first time in 40 years. Much to my surprise I was lionised in nearly every city I visited. People in the street even recognised me from the picture on the cover of *The Ugly Chinaman*. But because of the intellectual isolation and severe censorship imposed on China by the communist party over the years, Chinese people could only react to me in two ways: at one extreme, I was exalted as an all-knowing visionary and prophet, as China's saviour; at the other, I was excoriated as the lowest scum, and called a traitor to the Chinese people. A month ago, in December 1990, I was interviewed in Singapore. *The Straits Times* published a cover story about me, with a huge photo, entitled 'Bo Yang: The Ugly Chinaman'. Some things never change.

While I am pleased to be able to enjoy such a wide readership, my life as a writer has been something less than inspiring. Since 1950, I have published nearly 150 volumes of fiction, essays, poetry, reportage and history. My reportage has been made into a film. My history books are used as references in university courses. And my poetry and stories have been translated into foreign languages. But I never imagined that a book based on a talk I gave in which I criticised a few aspects of Chinese culture would stir up such a fuss among Chinese people all over the world. Interestingly enough, I discovered that regardless of whether they agreed or disagreed with me, all those who participated in the debate shared an admirably serious concern for the survival of Chinese culture. And it also became obvious that the enthusiasm they displayed in either railing against or defending Chinese culture greatly outweighed whatever interest they might have in literature or history. For an author this was a rather uncomfortable discovery.

I do not believe that the Chinese people are inherently inferior to anyone. In fact, if I thought that they were intellectually backward I would be the first to say so. The Tiananmen Square incident provided the Chinese people with an opportunity to show the world their true colours—their enthusiasm, warm-heartedness, discipline, kindness and consideration for others. For a few weeks during the spring of 1989, Beijing was a city of love. And for a while it looked as if everything I had written in *The Ugly Chinaman* was about to be disproven: *The Ugly Chinaman* was looking more and more like a ridiculous, slanderous tract. But then on the night of June 4, Beijing returned to 'normal'.

Are the Chinese people cursed? Are they condemned to an endless cycle of retrogression and recovery, recovery and retrogression? Ages ago, all the ethical tendencies and native wisdom of the Chinese people were crushed by the destructive elements of Confucian culture and despotic government, and gradually the remains were reconstituted in the biggest soy paste vat ever created in the history of human civilisation. If that wasn't enough, the coup de grace came in the 1950s, when the most corrosive elements of socialism—the system of public ownership and the cult of worshipping the leadership—infected the Chinese people with an international cultural virus, and left them gasping for breath. How different are the Chinese from the people of Eastern Europe, who have woken from a long bad dream to a world where democracy offers them a chance for a new life?

The harsh treatment *The Ugly Chinaman* received at the hands of the communists has finally brought this book to the attention of Western readers, and now it is appearing in English. Western readers should understand that this book represents a painful awakening for the Chinese people, as they acquire the courage to face their own shortcomings. If this book fails to make Western readers aware of the problems facing China, and leaves them with the impression that I have only written it in order to make fun of the Chinese, that not only spells disaster for me, but may have disastrous consequences for the Chinese people and the rest of the civilised world as well. To commit that mistake is to write off the ongoing struggle of this huge mass of people to escape from their tragic predicament and seek self-understanding.

The Tiananmen Square incident showed the world in a striking way what the Chinese people are capable of achieving when they are freed from their political shackles. But the rusty fetters of traditional Chinese culture cannot be discarded so easily. It will take the re-establishment of a market economy, the institution of a democratic system of government, and a long period of political and economic stability before the Chinese people can begin to live normal, healthy lives.

Every country has its bad times and its own history of shame. While China is no exception to this rule, China's bad times seem to have lasted for an extraordinarily long time. But when face-saving Chinese people start calling their compatriots 'Ugly Chinaman' in public, this marks the birth of a new era in which the Chinese may be able to gradually free themselves of their own ugliness. It is my fervent hope that Western readers will give the Chinese people their support and their blessings. For this they will be most grateful.

Bo Yang
Taipei, 25 January 1991

Translators' introduction

Few readers of this book are likely to have encountered a Chinese soy paste vat, but they will probably find the Ugly Chinaman remarkably familiar. This hypothetical creature, who bears the cross of 5000 years of Chinese civilisation, is the creation of Guo Yidong, who was born in Kaifeng, China, in 1920. After his expulsion from university in Manchuria for anti-communist activities, Guo worked as a journalist and teacher in Mukden and Peking, and fled to Taiwan in 1949, on the eve of the communist takeover. In his first decade on the island, Guo wrote fiction and poetry and worked as a teacher and journalist. Much of his writing was anti-communist in nature, and he became associated with the Chinese Youth Anti-Communist National Salvation Corps, founded in 1952 by Chiang Ching-kuo, the son of Chiang Kai-shek, 'to mobilise and train young people for the move back to the mainland'.

The late 1950s and early 1960s saw the revival in Taiwan of a form of satirical essay (*zawen*) associated with one of the greatest modern Chinese writers, Lu Xun (1881–1936). Writing essays in this genre under the *nom de plume* of Bo Yang (literally 'cypress and poplar', trees regarded by the Chinese as being able to survive harsh climates), Guo Yidong became a spokesperson for the Taiwanese, pointing his critical pen at such targets as human foibles, government corruption and police brutality.

One of the major themes of Bo Yang's essays takes up a debate in China that dates back to the mid-nineteenth century, the face-off between conservative advocates of traditional Chinese values on the one hand, and pro-Western reformists and modernisers on the other. As the reformers saw it, it was the 'spiritual civilisation' of Asia that was keeping China stuck firmly in the middle ages; China had to come to terms with the 'material civilisation' of the West. For China to become a strong, modern nation, it was believed, she had to discard her notions of spiritual superiority and share in the achievements of modern science.

Bo Yang was a moderate in this debate. He advocated democracy and modernisation for China, but was opposed to wholesale Westernisation, which he believed would create as many problems as it would solve. In his satirical essays written in the late 1960s, Bo Yang introduced the colourful notion of the culture of the soy paste vat as a metaphor for all the ills of Chinese society, past and present. Fulfilling the prescribed role of the outspoken Chinese intellectual, Bo Yang came down hard on present-day China. And the Kuomintang (KMT) authorities, playing their role as intolerant despots, retaliated.

The KMT had long been seeking an opportunity to silence this gadfly on the Chinese body politic, whose writing had won him as many enemies as friends on the provincial island. In 1967 Bo Yang obtained the rights to translate and publish the American comic strip series 'Popeye the Sailor' in Chinese. Popeye is a gritty-voiced straight-talker who touts spinach for its ability to inspire courage and defends the rights of the little guy. In the comic strip that brought Bo Yang down, Popeye has just bought an island, and goes there with his son to admire it. Here is a translation of the text, which Bo Yang toned down considerably from the original:

> *Popeye* What a beautiful kingdom. I am king; I am president; I can be anything I want to be.
> *Junior* What about me?
> *Popeye* Oh, you can be crown prince.
> *Junior* If I am going to be anything at all, I'm going to be president.
> *Popeye* Your tone of voice is rather bold for one who's just a baby.
> *Junior* But there are just two of us in the whole country, don't you know?
> *Popeye* My country is a democratic country; everyone has the right to vote.
> *Junior* Everyone? But there are just the two of us. Wait, let me think. I'll run for election too.
> *Popeye* Let me first make my election speech . . . Fellow-countrymen. . .
> *Junior* Not a bad beginning!
> *Popeye* You must not under any circumstances vote for Junior!
> *Junior* Hey! What's the big idea?*

---

* NOTE: This translation and much of the information here is drawn from Edel Lancashire, 'Popeye and the Case of Guo Yidong, Alias Bo Yang', *The China Quarterly* (London) No. 92, December 1982

This veiled attack on Chiang Kai-shek and his son Chiang Ching-kuo led to Bo Yang's arrest in March 1968. Over the next several weeks, the police interrogated Bo Yang about his communist connections in all-night sessions that wore him down to the point where he confessed to complicity with the communists—something he had been duped into believing would lead to his release. But Bo Yang had fallen into the KMT's trap, and under the cover of a media blackout, a military court charged him with being a communist agent and sentenced him to eighteen years in prison. Needless to say, the charge against him was an even more subtle fabrication than his confession.

Bo Yang's pen did not remain idle for long. He spent his nine-year sojourn in prison, his second decade on Taiwan, reading Chinese history and writing several long works on the subject. When he obtained an early release in 1977 at the age of 57, Taiwan and mainland China were entering a period of unprecedented political (in Taiwan's case) and economic liberalisation. The new climate of openness was one factor in Bo Yang's comeback as a controversial essayist, and paved the way for the birth of the Ugly Chinaman, Bo Yang's notorious sidekick during his third decade in Taiwan.

The text of this book, with the exception of one newspaper article, is drawn from Bo Yang's anthology, *The Ugly Chinaman*, published in Taipei in 1985.* The book consists of two parts. The first contains the 'keynote' spech entitled 'The Ugly Chinaman' that Bo Yang delivered at the University of Iowa in September 1984, a number of other speeches and interviews, and selections on topics related to the Ugly Chinaman theme drawn from Bo Yang's previously published essays. The second part consists of counter-attacks, repartees and 'condolences' by other Chinese writers in Taiwan, China, Hong Kong and the United States.

The present volume is divided into three sections. The first contains transcriptions of three major speeches about the Ugly Chinaman and an interview with Bo Yang. The second, 'Signs and symptoms of Chinese cultural senility', consists of selections from Bo Yang's other writings on the subject. The third, 'Waves breaking on the shore: an Ugly Chinaman forum', is our selection of articles written in response to Bo Yang's speech, 'The Ugly Chinaman'.

Bo Yang's extemporary and anecdotal speeches are a mixture of popular psychology, political analysis, story telling and humour. Bo Yang is constantly urging his Chinese compatriots to 'know themselves' in the Socratic, as well as the Buddhist way. Having rubbed the belly fur of the Confucian fuddy-duddies inhabiting the corridors of power

* *Choulou de Zhongguoren* Taipei: Lin bai Publishing Company

the wrong way, Bo Yang underwent a catharsis of his own in prison, where he paid the price for *not* being an Ugly Chinaman.

Bo Yang's various books on the subject of the Ugly Chinaman have sold remarkably well in the Asian market: over 200 000 copies in Taiwan, 40 000 in Hong Kong, 150 000 in Japan, and more than 400 000 in mainland China. There is also a Korean translation.

We have pruned some but not all of the repetition from the texts and eliminated a few of the more obscure references, but have left intact the rest in order to give readers a taste of the soy paste vat: something ancient, musty, cloying and vaguely familiar.

The chatty, contentious language of these speeches and essays appears easy to translate at first glance, but like the act of translation itself, can sometimes be fiendishly deceptive. Translations are bedevilled by split loyalties: on the one hand, fidelity to the text, in this case one written in a difficult, truly foreign language; and on the other, an obligation to the reader, who should be spared the eyesores and sour notes that accumulate in the translators' workshop. The present translation consciously errs on the side of the latter; were we only less visible.

We are grateful to Stephanie Holmes of Hong Kong for pointing out numerous Ugly Translator infelicities, but remain responsible for all the dissonance. Many thanks, too, to John Minford, who helped to bring the Ugly Chinaman alive in English during a few fondly remembered years in Hong Kong before the Ugly Chinaman took over.

A final word of warning. Ugly Chinamen tend to thrive in Chinese society, but are not exclusive to it. In fact, you don't have to be Chinese to be one.

Don J. Cohn
Jing Qing

Chek Nai Ping
Hong Kong
November 1991

In consultation with a doctor in The Land of the Soy Paste Vat

Once upon a time, there was country called The Land of the Soy Paste Fermentation Vat, known in short as Soyvat. The national pastime of this country was to debate on a daily basis about whether the country was indeed a soy paste vat, with the most hotly contested arguments taking place between doctors and their patients. Of course the doctors always lost. Below we recount a typical argument.

Patient I'm getting married next month. There'll be a big wedding party. Of course you're invited, I want you to be my guest of honour. What about the results of my last tests?

Doctor I am afraid I've got some bad news for you. The results are right here; you've got tertiary tuberculosis. The first stage was your coughing . . .

Patient That's pretty weird. You tell me that I have a cough, but you just coughed too. Does that mean you have TB as well?

Doctor My coughing is different from yours.

Patient How can that be? You're rich, you're smart, you graduated from university, you've drunk Amazon River water, you belong to a superior race, isn't that so?

Doctor I wouldn't say that. You also get feverish at night . . .

Patient If I don't say things like that, how else can I make you happy? As for my fever at night, my electric fan heats up whenever I turn it on, and by midnight it's hot enough to raise welts all over my hands when I touch it. Perhaps it's my fan that has TB, not me.

Doctor (*explains patiently*) Spitting up blood is another symptom . . .

Patient There's a dentist next door to where I live. Every patient he works on ends up spitting blood. Are you telling me every one of those people has tertiary TB too?

Doctor   Of course not, I'm just talking in general . . .

Patient   All right then, let's go back to the beginning. If I do have TB, even seventh- or eighth-stage TB, what difference does it make? Is it really worth making such a big fuss about it? Don't people in foreign countries get TB all the time? Why do you have to pick on me? I'm getting married next month, it's a secret so far. Why can't you give me a word or two of encouragement, instead of attacking me? Do you have any good reason to despise me, or to seek revenge? Or maybe it's that you want to break up my upcoming marriage?

Doctor   I'm afraid you misunderstand me completely, all I wanted to say was that . . .

Patient   No, no, I understand everything you're saying very clearly. In fact, I can see right through your lungs. Your mother died when you were young, so you didn't get enough love when you were growing up. Later, you spent many years in jail for robbery and rape. You have no respect for the law, you can't tolerate other people being happy, or a foreign country enjoying honour or glory.

Doctor   Aren't you taking this a bit too far?

Patient   No, this is very much to the point. Tell me the truth now. How did you actually murder that old lady, even though she was so kind to you?

Doctor   (*somewhat nervously*) Your diagnosis is based on a blood and sputum test, how could I possibly fake the results?

Patient   I know you're not faking the results, just like you'll never be able to fake the way you plunged the knife into that old lady's chest. All the progressive and patriotic people in this country have had enough of your insults. I know the way you despise all of your fellow countrymen from the bottom of your heart. You've diagnosed every single one of them as suffering from tertiary TB. Aren't you ashamed of yourself?

Doctor   My dear friend, I am only concerned with your well-being, and hope that you will recover soon. I really have no bad feelings for you. Otherwise why would I tell you the truth about your condition?

Patient   (*sneering and coughing*) You're a bloody executioner, that's what you are. All the honest, patriotic people in this country will get together and do something to stop you from murdering the Motherland, although you claim to be acting out of 'love'.

Doctor   My diagnosis is based on scientific evidence, such as the results of your sputum test. In fact the test was carried out at Hindustan University.

Patient   You're nothing but a foreign bootlicker, a bloody xenophiliac. You're a scoundrel, a thug. You've already destroyed our national self esteem. I'm warning you, you'll pay a stiff price for your blatant xenophilia!

Doctor (*with courage*) Cut out the nonsense, will you? Look, there's no escaping now, you can't use sticks and stones and dirty names to take the place of reason. What does my past behaviour and our conversation today have to do with each other? What matters here is whether or not you have TB.

Patient Here you go again, playing the 'Ugly Chinaman'. You're full of rubbish. We all know your background, it's obvious you're rotten to the core. Of course there's a relationship between your past and the present. It's people like you who are to blame for China's problems. You make foreigners look down on Chinese people because you give them the idea that we're all suffering from TB. Traitors like you suck the blood of the Chinese people and kiss the arses of the barbarian devils. God will strike you dead! Imperial court guards! (*coughs*) Take him away!

Of course this scenario doesn't really require imperial court guards (although Bo Yang was taken away once in precisely that manner). Sometimes you get beaten up with clubs, other times they attack you with pen and ink.

23 July 1985

PART I
Bo Yang speaks

The Ugly Chinaman

Speech given at Iowa University, 24
September 1984

For many years I've contemplated writing a book called *The Ugly Chinaman*. When the novel *The Ugly American* was published in the United States, the US State Department chose it as a guide to policy making. But when the Japanese ambassador to Argentina published a book called *The Ugly Japanese*, he was immediately recalled from his post. This is a good example of the gap that separates the East and the West. In China, for sure, things would be much worse. If I wrote a book called *The Ugly Chinaman*, you would soon be delivering me my meals in jail. In Taiwan, prisoners pay for their own food, which is the main reason why I haven't written such a book yet. For many years, however, I have been looking for an opportunity to speak about this subject in public, and to provide Chinese people in all walks of life with some food for thought—if not condemnation. Talking about this subject in public is no easy matter either. A group of people in Taipei once invited me to speak on this subject but when they heard the title of my speech, the invitation was swiftly withdrawn. Thus I am proud to say that this is the very first time I have lectured in public on the subject of 'The Ugly Chinaman'. I would like to thank all of you present for giving me this precious opportunity.

Once I was invited by Tunghai University (in Taichung, Taiwan) to give a lecture. I told the chairman of the Student Association there that the topic would be 'The Ugly Chinaman' and asked him if he foresaw any problems. Though he assured me there would be none, I insisted: 'You'd better ask the Dean's Office. I myself am already something of a problem, and if I start talking about a touchy subject, that makes two counts against me.'

After consulting with the Dean's Office he telephoned me. 'Nothing

3

serious, though they wondered if you wouldn't mind changing the title of your speech. The Dean's Office thinks it's a bit too direct.' He then gave me a long and very high-sounding title and asked me what I thought of it.

'I don't like it one bit, but if you have to change it, go ahead and do it!' That was the first time I had spoken in public about 'The Ugly Chinaman'. When I asked the chairman of the Student Association to record the lecture so I could transcribe it later and turn it into an article, he readily agreed. But when I received the tape, I discovered that the entire tape was blank except for the first few sentences.

I am 65 years old now. Some friends of mine in Taipei held a birthday party for me on 7 March. I told them, 'I've been around for 65 years now, and every one of those years has been an ordeal for me'. This ordeal was not my own personal trials and tribulations, but rather those of Chinese everywhere. Most of you young people here, especially those of you from Taiwan, have grown up in a relatively prosperous society. The concept of 'ordeal' may grate on your ears, or be difficult for you to believe, and perhaps even more difficult for you to understand. The ordeals I refer to are not personal hardships or political crises, but rather problems that transcend the sphere of the individual and the realm of politics. They are issues that involve all the Chinese people. I'm not talking about a particular individual's suffering, or even about the anguish of my own generation. The point I want to make is: if we don't come to grips with this suffering and all the destructive elements in Chinese culture, they will continue to wreak havoc upon us and our descendants forever.

How shameful it is to be Chinese

Ninety per cent of the refugees in the Khao-i-dang Refugee Camp in Thailand are Chinese (by blood or cultural background, not nationality) who have been expelled from Vietnam, Kampuchea or Laos. A few years ago, a female student from the Overseas Chinese Institute of the College of Chinese Culture in Taiwan joined an aid team which went to Thailand to work with the refugees there. But she became so upset there that she returned home after a few days. When I spoke to her about her experiences, she was in tears: 'It was so miserable there. I couldn't stand it any longer.'

The situation of the Chinese refugees in Thailand is indeed pathetic. For example, Chinese people in the camp are not permitted to own any property or enter into any form of business. If, for instance, your shirt has a hole in it, and you 'pay' the old lady next door half a bowl of rice to sew it for you, this is considered 'business'. And if the authorities find out about it, they will possibly force the old lady to remove all of her clothing in front of them, and then take her to the local magistrate's office, where they will ply her with questions like, 'Why did you break the law?' Under these circumstances, she can be considered fortunate. While making me angry and upset, the thought of such insulting behaviour also makes me wonder: what evil acts have Chinese committed that they should end up being punished in this way?

Two years ago, my wife and I were in Paris. Coming out of a Metro station, I noticed a middle-aged Asian woman selling jewellery from a little stand in the street. My wife and I were chatting in Chinese as we looked over her wares, and when she joined the conversation, it made us feel right at home. I asked her how she was able to speak Chinese. She turned out to be a Chinese who had escaped from Vietnam and had lived for a while in the Khao-i-dang camp. She began sobbing, and I tried to comfort her: 'Things are better for you now. At least you're not starving.' As we turned to leave, she sighed, 'How shameful it is to be Chinese!' That's one sigh I will never forget for the rest of my life.

In the nineteenth century, many parts of the East Indies, which we now call Southeast Asia, were either Dutch or British colonies. A British commissioner who lived in Malaysia at that time wrote the following: 'The lives of the Chinese in the nineteenth century were filled with calamity and disaster'. He had seen the Chinese in the East Indies living like pigs. They were uneducated and illiterate, cut off from the rest of society, and constantly in danger of being slaughtered.

Actually, the Chinese in China are worse off today than they were in the nineteenth century. The most depressing thing is how, over the past hundred years, almost every hope that the Chinese people have embraced has gone up in smoke. And whenever a fresh hope appears on the horizon, promising some improvement in people's lives, it invariably ends up causing them great disappointment and making the situation worse. And when another hope appears, promising similar progress, it too ends up bringing in its wake only further disillusionment, greater disappointment and more horrendous disasters.

A country is a relatively permanent institution, while an individual's life is limited. How much hope can an individual have in his lifetime? How many dreams can be shattered in a lifetime? Does the future hold promise? Or will it bring disappointment? There can be no conclusive answers to these questions. Once when I was lecturing in New York and relating a particularly painful incident, someone in the audience said, 'You come from Taiwan. You ought to be inspiring us, giving us hope, and fostering our patriotism. I never imagined you would end up making us feel depressed and discouraged.'

I don't deny that people need constant encouragement and inspiration. The problem is, once you inspire Chinese people, where do they go from there? I've been given all sorts of encouragement and inspiration ever since I was a child. When I was five or six years old, grown ups would tell me, 'The future of China is in your generation's hands'. At the time, that seemed like a very heavy burden to bear all by myself. But only a few years later, I was telling my son, 'The future of China is in your generation's hands'. Now my son is telling his son, 'The future of China . . .' How many more generations will this go on for?

On the Chinese mainland, the Anti-Rightist Campaign in 1958 was followed by the decade of the Cultural Revolution, a disaster unprecedented in the history of human civilisation. The Cultural Revolution not only left millions dead, it also crushed humanitarian values and defiled the sanctity of the human spirit, without which there remains very little to separate men and beasts. During China's 'ten-year holocaust' people behaved like animals. Can an entire nation of moral degenerates be saved?

Over 30 per cent of the population of Malaysia is Chinese. But in a museum I visited when I was there, the labels describing the exhibits were in Malay and English only. I'm not suggesting that they must have Chinese labels, or that it's a bad thing that they don't. I mention this merely to point out the narrow-mindedness of the Malaysians, and to show how the Chinese in Malaysia have very little influence or prestige, and are not respected by the majority. A Thai Chinese I know claimed that the Chinese control the vital rice market in Thailand. This is mere self-deception. (The Thai Chinese are active in the rice business, but can they claim to 'control' that vital market?) I advised him to stop flattering himself in this regard. One command from the top and everything they have could be taken away from them.

Everyone is talking about the Hong Kong question these days. It's a shameful thing for one country to snatch away another country's territory. And when that territory is returned to its rightful owner—like a child returning to its mother's embrace—it should be a cause for celebration on both sides. Do you recall France's ceding of Alsace Lorraine to Germany? Losing these two states came as a terrible blow to France, but the eventual reunification was a cause for great rejoicing. In the case of Hong Kong, however, no sooner was the news announced that the British were going to return the territory to the Chinese Motherland than people panicked en masse. Why?

In Taiwan, a number of young people—both native Taiwanese and mainlanders—support the idea of an independent Taiwan. I remember how happy everyone was when Japan handed Taiwan back to China in 1945; indeed we felt like lost children finding our way back to our mother's warm embrace. What has happened over the past five decades to make this child want to leave home again, and try to make it on its own?

Take Cyprus, for example, which is split up between the Turks and the Greeks, who differ in terms of language, ethnicity and religion. If the Turks can get along with 'aliens' on that island, why can't we Chinese get along with our own kind? Chinese people share the same blood, similar looks, identical ancestry and culture, the same language; the major differences are merely geographical.

The circumstances described above not only make it extremely difficult to be Chinese, but also cause us untold shame and injury. Even the Chinese community in the United States is plagued by the absurd situation in which leftists, rightists, moderates, independents, left-leaning moderates, moderate-leaning leftists, right-leaning moderates, and moderate-leaning rightists all seem to lack a common language for discourse, and are constantly lurching at each other's throats with the passion of a vendetta.

What does this say about the Chinese people? And what does this imply about China? No other civilisation on earth has such a long history or well-preserved cultural tradition, a tradition that at certain times has given rise to the most advanced civilisation in the world. Neither the Greeks nor the Egyptians of today bear any relationship to their ancient forebears, while Chinese today are the direct descendants of the ancient Chinese. How have such a great people and nation degenerated into such ugliness? Not only have foreigners bullied us; what is worse, for centuries we've been tormented by our own kind—from tyrannical emperors to despotic officials and ruthless mobs.

On my visits to the United States and Europe, I've especially enjoyed watching children playing in the parks. They seem so happy, uninhibited and well adjusted that it makes me jealous. In Taiwan, on the other hand, every child who goes to school has to wear glasses to correct their myopia, and in order to cope with the pressure of schoolwork, many children grow aloof and arrogant. A woman faints and collapses at home, but when her son tries to help her, she shouts at him, 'Let me die! Don't bother with me! Do your homework! Do your homework!'

When my wife was teaching in Taiwan, whenever she started lecturing to her students about morality or personal values, they would immediately raise a protest: 'We don't want to learn about how to live, we want to learn how to get high marks on our examinations.' But this is nothing compared with children on the Chinese mainland, who grow up learning how to fight with each other, subject each other to psychological torture in 'struggle' sessions, cheat and swindle, and betray their parents and friends. Is this the purpose of an education? I tremble to think what will happen when this generation grows up.

Chinese people are the same everywhere

I have lived in Taiwan for the past three decades. I spent the first decade writing fiction, the second writing essays and the last in jail—quite a nice balance. I no longer write fiction because fiction only deals indirectly with real problems through the medium of form and characters, while essays are daggers that can pierce the hearts of scoundrels and villains.

Writing essays is like sitting in a car next to the driver, telling him when he makes a wrong turn, warning him to stay in the slow lane and not pass, to watch out for the bridge ahead, to reduce speed, to beware the approaching intersection, and to heed red lights. After exhorting and teaching drivers for many years, someone must have decided that I had taught enough, because I ended up in jail. People in power think that as long as no one is around to point out their errors, then they can't possibly do anything wrong.

During my incarceration I spent many long hours contemplating my fate. What crimes had I committed? What laws had I broken? I continued to ponder these questions after my release from prison and began to wonder whether I was a special case. On this trip to Iowa, when I have had the great fortune to meet writers from mainland China, I discovered that God has predestined people like myself to end up in jail, whether the jail be in Taiwan or in mainland China. One of these mainland writers told me, 'Someone like you would never have survived the Red Guards and the Cultural Revolution. In fact, they would have snuffed you out during the Anti-Rightist Movement.'

Why must Chinese people who have the guts to speak the truth suffer so terribly? I have asked a number of people from the mainland why they ended up in prison. Their answer was, 'Because I said a few things that happened to be true'. And that's the way it is. But why does telling the truth land one in such unfortunate circumstances? The way I see it, this is not a personal problem, but a fundamental flaw in Chinese culture.

A few days ago I had a discussion with the party secretary of the 'All-China Writers Association'. He made me so angry that I literally was unable to speak. I used to think I could hold my own in an argument; but this guy knocked the breath out of me before I knew what had hit me. I can't blame him for this, though, the same way I don't blame the cops who handled my case in Taipei. If you lived in their world and were conversant with their ways, you would probably act just like they do, and believe that what you were doing was right. I would do the same thing, though I would probably be even more obnoxious than that party secretary. People often say, 'Your future is in your own hands'. Approaching the end of my life, I don't believe that any more. Only about half of your life is in your own hands. Other people control the rest.

Life is a little bit like a stone in a cement mixer; when it gets tossed around with the other ingredients, it loses control of its own existence. I could cite similar analogies *ad infinitum*, but the conclusion I always come to is that the problems of the Chinese people are not individual but rather social and cultural problems. Before he died, Jesus said, 'Forgive them, for they know not what they do'. When I first heard that statement as a child, I thought it rather bland and frivolous, and as I grew older I continued to feel that it lacked substance. Only now do I appreciate its profundity and bitter irony. Jesus' words taught me that the Chinese people's ugliness grows out of our own ignorance of the fact that we are ugly.

Because Taiwan and the United States have broken off diplomatic relations, the expenses for our trip to the United States were borne by Iowa University and Pei Zhuzhang, the owner of the Yenching Restaurant in Iowa City. Pei is a Chinese–American who had never set foot in China, nor met me before. His generosity moved me deeply. He said, 'Before reading your books, I felt that the Chinese people were a great people. After reading them my thinking changed entirely. Your books inspired me and made me want to hear you speak in person.'

When Mr Pei started thinking about Chinese culture and its problems, he wondered if there were some basic defects in the moral fibre of the Chinese people. Before I travelled abroad for the first time, Professor Sun Kuan-han said to me, 'When you come back to Taiwan, there is one thing I absolutely forbid you to say to me, and that is: "Chinese people are the same everywhere" ', so I promised him that I would not say it. But when I got back to Taiwan and he asked me about my trip, the first thing I said was, 'You warned me not to say it, but: Chinese people are the same everywhere!'

Sun hoped that with time the Chinese people would change and mature, and he found it hard to imagine that this would never happen. Are there innate flaws in the Chinese people? When God created the Chinese, did he make us so ugly on purpose?

I believe that there is nothing inherently wrong with the Chinese national character. I am not saying this out of self-pity. Nor are Chinese people lacking in intelligence. Every university in the United States has Chinese students at the top of their class, and we have produced numerous noted scientists: Sun Kuan-han, the father of Chinese nuclear physics and Nobel Prize winners C. N. Yang and C. T. Lee. The Chinese character is not fundamentally flawed, and I am sure that we have the ability to make China a healthy and happy place to live. I also believe that China will some day become a great nation. But we must not spend all of our time and energy trying to make China a major military power. It is infinitely more important to bring some happiness into people's lives. Once we achieve this, we can concern ourselves with power and greatness. We must also ask why, over the last century, have we so often failed to free ourselves from suffering?

The virus of traditional Chinese culture

I am going to risk proposing a comprehensive diagnosis for the problems mentioned above: Chinese culture is infected with a virus which has been transmitted from generation to generation and which today still resists cure. People say that if you are a failure, you can blame your ancestors, but there is a significant flaw in this argument. In Ibsen's play *Ghosts*, a syphilitic couple give birth to a syphilitic son, who has to take medicine every time his illness flares up. At one point in the drama, the son exclaims, 'I never asked you for life. And what sort of a life have you given me?'*

Can we blame the son, and not blame his parents? We Chinese should neither blame our parents nor our ancestors, but rather the culture that our ancestors have bequeathed us. This huge country, with one quarter of the world's population, is a pit of quicksand filled with poverty, ignorance, strife and bloodshed, a pit from which it cannot extricate itself. When I observe the way people in other countries carry on interpersonal relations, I envy them. The traditional culture of China has conferred upon the Chinese a wide range of unseemly characteristics.

Three of the most notorious characteristics are filth, sloppiness and noisiness. In Taipei they once tried to mount a campaign against filth and disorder, but it only lasted a few days. Our kitchens and our homes are always in a mess. In many residential areas, as soon as the Chinese move in, everyone else moves out. A young woman I know, a college

---

* *Ghosts and Other Plays* translated by Peter Watts, Middlesex and Baltimore: Penguin Books, 1964, p. 100

graduate, married a Frenchman and moved to Paris. Soon their home became a regular stopping-off place for her friends who were travelling in Europe. She told me that as more and more Asians (not all of them Chinese) started to move into the building, the French started to move out. This is a terribly disturbing thought. But when I went to Paris and saw the place for myself, there were ice-cream wrappers and sandals strewn about everywhere, children running and yelling in the halls, and graffiti covering the walls. The whole place smelled like a mouldy cellar as well. I asked her, 'Can't you organise all the residents and clean the place up?' She replied, 'It's impossible. The French are not the only people who think we are filthy slobs; after living here like this, we feel the same way.'

Turning to the subject of noise, Chinese people's voices must be the loudest on earth, with the Cantonese taking the gold medal. I heard a joke about this: Two Cantonese men in the United States are having a conversation in the street. An American walks by and thinks they are having a fight, so he calls the police. When the police arrive and ask them what they are fighting about, they say, 'We're just whispering'.

Why do Chinese people shout when they talk? Because we are insecure by nature. The louder we shout, the more right we are. If we shout at the top of our lungs, we must be right, otherwise why expend so much energy? The above-mentioned behaviour patterns are damaging to both our self-image and our mental equilibrium. Filth, sloppiness and noisiness can also damage our nerves. If Chinese lived in a clean, orderly environment, they might behave entirely differently.

The scourge of infighting

Chinese people are notorious for quarrelling and squabbling among themselves. A Japanese person all by himself is no better than a pig, but three Japanese together are as awesome as a dragon. The Japanese people's ability to co-operate makes them nearly invincible, and in neither commerce nor war can the Chinese ever dream of competing with them. If three Japanese people in the same business are in Taipei together, they will take turns making sales. Chinese businessmen in the same situation would act like perfect Ugly Chinamen. If Li is selling something for $50, Ma will offer it for $40; if Li lowers the price to $30, Ma will cut it to $20. Every Chinaman is a dragon in his own right.

Chinese people can be extremely convincing when they talk, thanks to their remarkably nimble tongues. If you believe what they say, there is nothing they cannot do, including extinguishing the sun with a single breath of air, and ruling the world with a single flick of the hand. In the laboratory or examination hall, where no personal relationships are involved, Chinese can produce impressive results. But when three fiery Chinese dragons get together, they can only produce about as much as a single pig, or a single insect, if that much. This is because of their addiction to infighting.

Chinese people squabble among themselves in every situation, since their bodies lack those cells that enable most human beings to get along with each other. When non-Chinese people criticise the Chinese for this weakness, I like to warn them, 'Chinese people are like this because God knows that with more than one billion of them, if they ever got their act together, the rest of the world wouldn't be able to handle them. God has been good to you foreigners by making it impossible for the Chinese to cooperate among themselves.' But it is very painful for me to say this.

Chinese people can easily come up with enough reasons for why they don't cooperate with each other to fill a book. The best example of this uncohesiveness can be found right here in the United States, where every Chinese community is divided up into as many factions as there are days in the year, each determined to choke the life out of the rest. There's an old Chinese saying: one monk drinks from the water bucket on his back; two monks drink from the water bucket they carry on a pole; three monks have no water to drink. Why do we need so many people to accomplish something so simple?

Chinese people simply don't understand the importance of cooperation. But if you tell a Chinaman he doesn't understand, he will sit down and write a book just for you entitled *The Importance of Co-operation*.

On my last visit to the United States, I stayed with a friend who teaches at an American university. He was a very reasonable and intelligent person, and we held discussions on many subjects, including how to save China. The following day I told this man that I wanted to visit a Mr G., a mutual acquaintance of ours. At the mere mention of Mr G.'s name, my friend's eyes lit up in anger. And when I asked him to drive me to Mr G.'s house, he said, 'Sorry, Bo Yang, you'll have to get there on your own'. Both Mr G. and my host are university professors and grew up in the same place in China, but they cannot tolerate each other. Are they rational human beings? I'll say it again: infighting is a serious problem among the Chinese.

Those of you who live in the United States know that the people who harass Chinese people the most are other Chinese, not Yankees. It takes a Chinaman to betray a Chinaman; only a Chinaman would have a good reason to frame or slander another Chinaman.

Here is one example: Shortly after he developed a coal mine in

Malaysia, a man I know was accused of several serious crimes. The plaintiff, it turned out, was an old friend of his. Both of them had left China at the same time and had started out in Malaysia with nothing in their pockets. When my friend asked his old acquaintance why he had done such a cruel thing, he said, 'We both started out together with nothing, but now you're a millionaire and I'm hardly getting by. If I don't sue *you*, who else can I sue?' This is one isolated incident, but it shows how Chinese people can be their own worst enemies.

To cite another example, in a country as big as the United States, where no individual amounts to much more than a drop in the ocean, how would anyone find out if you were an illegal immigrant? Only if someone went out of his way to turn you in to the immigration authorities. And who would do such a nasty thing for no good reason? Only one of your best friends, an Ugly Chinaman.

Many Chinese people in the United States have told me that if their boss is Chinese, they constantly have to be on their toes. Chinese bosses never promote their Chinese employees, and when people are being laid off, they are always the first to go. Such occasions give Chinese bosses golden opportunities to demonstrate their impartiality and sense of fairness.

Why do people constantly compare the Chinese with the Jews? Many say that the Chinese and the Jews are particularly industrious. We can approach this question from two angles. First, the industriousness which was once the great pride of the Chinese people was destroyed during the reign of the Gang of Four in the Cultural Revolution, as a result of which Chinese people no longer possess a virtue that sustained them for thousands of years.

How else can we compare ourselves with the Jews? Chinese newspapers often carry headlines describing how fierce arguments often break out in the Israeli parliament, the Knesset, with, for example, three leading politicians holding three entirely contrary views. But the same newspapers never mention that once a consensus is reached, the three of them will take the same course of action. And while that battle of words was taking place inside the Knesset, a real war was being fought outside, with the enemy surrounding the country on all sides—and yet the Israelis still held their elections. Everyone knows that in order to hold an election, you need an opposition party, otherwise an election is no better than a second-rate soap opera.

If three Chinese people with three different opinions reach a consensus, the three of them will still act according to their own will. For instance, Wang proposes going to New York and Chang wants to go to San Francisco. There is a vote and New York is chosen as the common destination. In Israel, everyone would go to New York. But in China, Chang would say, 'You can go to New York. I'm going to San Francisco'.

In a British film there was a scene in which several children were having an argument about whether to climb a tree or go swimming. After quarrelling for a while, they decided to vote. The majority chose to climb a tree, so they all climbed a tree. Simple though it seems, this left a deep impression on me. Democracy in the West is more than mere form; it is a regular part of daily life, while in China democracy is there purely for show. During elections, high officials in China insist on being photographed holding a ballot in their hands to show the world that they deign to take part in the democratic process. Democracy is not an intrinsic part of those officials' lives; it is all show.

A reluctance to admit error

Chinese people's inability to co-operate, and their predilection for bickering among themselves, are deep-rooted, harmful traits. These behaviour patterns cannot be traced to any inherent flaws in the Chinese national character, but rather are symptoms of an infection spread by the virus of traditional Chinese culture, that causes us to act in ways we can neither conceal nor control. We know that we fight among ourselves, yet it is beyond our control to stop it. 'If the pot breaks, nobody will have anything to eat; but if the sky falls, someone taller than me will be there to stop it from falling on my head. I don't have to lift a finger.'

The tendency towards internecine struggle has spawned another insidious phenomenon: an utter reluctance to admit mistakes. How many of you have ever heard a Chinese admit that he or she has made an error? If you have, then break out the Maotai: it is time to start celebrating the renaissance of China!

Once, many years ago, I spanked my daughter for something she had done wrong, but soon realised that I had made a mistake. Her crying made me feel terrible inside. She was a young and helpless thing, so my sudden turning against her must have given her a terrible shock. I picked her up and said, 'I'm sorry. Daddy made a big mistake. I promise you I'll never do it again. Be a good girl and accept Daddy's apology.' But she went on crying for a long time. Though this upset me greatly, I was also proud of the fact that I had admitted my error.

Chinese people are highly reluctant to admit their errors, and can produce a myriad of reasons to cover their mistakes. There's an old adage: 'Contemplate your faults behind closed doors'. Whose faults? The guy's next door, of course! When I was teaching school, I told my students to keep a diary and record their weekly activities. The entries read like this: 'Today Ming cheated me. I've always been good to him. It must be because I'm too kind to him and too honest.' But when I read Ming's diary, I saw that Ming thought that *he* was too kind and too honest as well. If everyone in the world is so kind and honest, can there be any dishonest people left?

Chinese people don't admit their mistakes because somewhere during their long evolution they lost the knack of it. Of course we can disavow our mistakes, but that won't make them disappear. To cover their mistakes, Chinese people go well out of their way and even commit additional mistakes, merely to cover their initial blunders. Thus it is often said that Chinese are addicted to bragging, boasting, lying, equivocating and, worst of all, slandering others. For years Chinese have been going on about the supreme greatness of China, and making extravagant claims about how Chinese culture can make the world a better place to live in. But because these daydreams never come true, all of this is pure rubbish.

I don't have to cite examples of boasting and lying, but Chinese verbal brutality deserves special mention. Even in the confines of the bedroom, where Western couples habitually address each other as 'honey' and 'darling', Chinese people prefer such endearments as 'You deserve death by a thousand cuts!' And in matters of politics or money, and in power struggles of any kind, Chinese people's spite knows no bounds. What makes Chinese people so mean and petty?

Stuck in the mud of bragging and boasting

A friend who used to write traditional adventure stories started a business. When I asked him whether he had made a lot of money, he told me, 'Are you kidding? I'm about ready to hang myself!' I asked him how he lost so much money. 'You can't imagine. It's a total waste of time talking with Chinese businessmen, you never know what they're really thinking.' Europeans and Americans have said to me, 'It's hard getting to know Chinese people. You never know what's on their minds.' I replied, 'You think you're the only one with that problem? When Chinese talk to each other, they have the same problem.'

One way of figuring out what is going on in a Chinese person's mind is to observe his or her body language and facial expression, and to cultivate the habit of beating around the bush yourself. You ask someone, 'Have you eaten dinner?' and the answer is 'Yes', but he is actually so hungry you can hear his stomach rumbling. In an election, a Western politician will say, 'I sincerely believe I am qualified for the post. Please vote for me.' But Chinese people prefer to take after Zhuge Liang: if offered a post, a modest Ugly Chinaman will decline the honour at least three times. 'Who, me? I'm hardly qualified for the post.' But if you take him literally and vote for someone else, he will never speak to you again.

To give another example, you invite me to give a lecture, and I say, 'Who, me? I'm a terrible public speaker.' But if you don't insist that I give that lecture, and we meet in the street in Taipei some day, I'll be sure to aim a brick at your head. If everyone acts in this manner, we will never mend our ways. The way things are now, it takes ten mistakes to cover up one mistake, and one hundred mistakes to cover up ten.

I was once visiting a British professor in Taichung, when a Chinese friend of mine teaching in the same university came in and invited me to dinner in his home that evening. I said, 'I'm sorry, I've already got an appointment for tonight.' He replied, 'That's all right, come anyway. I'll see you later.' Chinese speak to each other in this fashion all the time, but a Western person overhearing such an exchange will find it hard to know what is actually going on. When the British professor and I had finished our work, I said to him, 'I'm heading home.' He asked me, 'I thought you were going to your friend's home for dinner.' I said, 'Where did you get that idea?' 'But he's making dinner especially for you!' This is just one example of how difficult it is for Western people to understand the noncommittal etiquette practised by most Chinese.

The behaviour patterns described above give Chinese people a heavy cross to bear from birth. Rarely does a day go by when it isn't necessary to decipher what's going on in someone's mind. With friends, the problems are minimal. But when dealing with government officials or rich and powerful people you constantly have to read minds. What a waste of energy! Consider the popular Chinese saying: 'Getting things done is easy; dealing with people is hard'. Dealing with people brings us into the sphere of 'cultural software'. All of you who have lived abroad will be able to appreciate this. When you go back to China and want to get something done, two plus two equals four. But when you have to deal with other people, two plus two may equal five, or one or 853. If you tell the truth about something, others may accuse you of attacking or attempting to overthrow the government. This is a serious problem, and one which keeps the Chinese stuck in the muck of bragging, lying, boasting and slander.

I like to boast that I can sleep through any meeting or conference. This is only possible because no one who attends conferences says what they really believe. This habit of 'slinging the bull' is even more prevalent on the mainland than in Taiwan. One of the participants in this year's International Writers' Program at the University of Iowa was the mainland woman writer Shen Rong. The title of one of her books, which I highly recommend, is *Truth or Lies*.

The Chinese mentality makes us tell lies and act dishonestly. We should at least be able to recognise a bad thing when we see it. But when we glorify bad things or ignore them, it is a sign that our 'cultural software' has been invaded by a virus. Take theft, for example. No one can say that robbery is an ennobling act, but when people ignore it and cease to think of it as a dishonest act, we have reached a crisis. This is the crisis Chinese people are faced with today.

Modern Chinese have become increasingly narrowminded and closed off from the rest of the world because of their inability to admit their mistakes and their predilection for bragging, lying and slander.

What state of mind or philosophical outlook properly reflects China's vast territory and strikingly rich cultural heritage? Magnanimity, broadmindedness and worldliness come to mind. But where do you meet people with such qualities except in books or on TV? Have you ever met a Chinese who is truly magnanimous and openminded? In many situations, a single hostile glance will spur a Chinese gentleman to whip out his sword and flash it in your face. Then watch when it turns out you have divergent points of view. Westerners can shake hands after a fight, but Chinese become enemies for life, and will even perpetuate a vendetta for three generations. Why do Chinese lack tolerance for others?

Narrow-mindedness and intolerance result in an unbalanced personality constantly wavering between two extremes: chronic inferiority on the one hand, and overbearing arrogance on the other. A Chinese with an inferiority complex is a slave; a Chinese with a superiority complex is a tyrant. As individuals, Chinese lack self-respect. In the inferiority mode, they feel like a heap of dog shit, so the closer they get to influential people, the wider their smiles. In the arrogant mode, everyone else is a heap of dog shit. These radical swings in self-esteem make Chinese people imbalanced creatures with psychotic tendencies.

A nation of inflation

In Chinese society it is easy to astound people by performing miracles, but impossible to sustain such activity for an extended period. As soon as someone can claim some trivial achievement, he will suddenly lose his hearing or eyesight, or have difficulty walking. Anyone who publishes two articles is an 'author'. Anyone who acts in two films is a 'star'. Anyone who is a petty bureaucrat for two years is 'the people's saviour'. A student who spends two years in a university in the United States is a 'returned overseas scholar'. Such titles are all auto-inflationary.

Several years ago a terrible traffic accident took place in Taiwan. A bus carrying a group of fourth-year students from Taiwan Normal University was passing through the most dangerous section of the Cross-Island Highway, when the conductress announced: 'Our driver today is one of the best in Taiwan. Look how young, strong and handsome he is!' To prove this, he took his hands off the steering wheel and responded to the students' applause with the traditional clasped-hands salute. I don't have to tell you what happened next. This is boasting at its worst: he was such an accomplished driver that he didn't even have to steer.

I once saw a film which told the story of a man who had invented a pair of 'flying wings' and was ordered by the emperor to give a flying demonstration. The man showed his wings to the crowd, and was about to climb up the tower from which he was to take off, when the crowd's thunderous applause fired his self-confidence to the point where he threw down his wings and declared he would fly without them. At this point, his wife stepped in and tried to deter him from going ahead with his preposterous scheme: 'What do you think you're doing? You can't fly without your wings!' He turned to her angrily and said, 'What do you know!' When she began to climb up the tower to stop him, he stepped on her fingers. Reaching the top of the tower, he closed the hatch and took off. Seconds later there was a loud thud, and then silence. The crowd suddenly exploded in anger. 'We paid good money to see him fly, not to watch him plunge to his death!' and demanded that the dead man's wife fly for them. She had no choice but to comply. In her grief, before jumping, the woman addressed her husband's departed soul: 'You and your big ideas, you've killed yourself and your wife as well'.

What makes the Chinese people prone to self-inflation? Consider the saying, 'A small vessel is easily filled'. Due to inveterate narrow-mindedness and arrogance, even the slightest success makes an Ugly Chinaman feel that the world is too small to contain him. It is tolerable if a few people behave in this manner, but if the entire population, or a majority behave this way, and they all happen to be Chinese, it spells disaster for China. Because Chinese have never had much self-respect, it is immensely difficult for them to treat others as equals. There are two alternatives: either you are my master, or my slave. This makes people narrow-minded, and reluctant to admit mistakes. Being wrong all the time has made the Chinese paranoid.

Here is one example. A man I knew in Taipei became critically ill and was admitted to the prestigious Central Clinic, where a doctor saved his life only after sticking innumerable tubes into him. Two or three days later, the members of his family moved him to Veterans Hospital, mainly because the fees at the Central Clinic were so high. When the doctor in charge of the case learned about this, he exploded: 'I went to great lengths to save your life, and now you want to go to another hospital'. He then started to disconnect the life-supporting tubes from the patient, who nearly died as a result.

My friend told me this story with a mixture of sadness and anger. I told him, 'Give me that doctor's name, and I'll write an article about the terrible way he treated you'. But he nearly panicked and upbraided me: 'You've got ants in your pants, Bo Yang. If I had known you were such a busy-body, I wouldn't have told you the story in the first place.' I nearly blew up at this point. 'He's only a doctor, what are you afraid of? If you get sick again and don't go to him, do you think he's going to go to your house and treat you, just to get his revenge? If he really wants his revenge, he'll go after me, not you, since I'm the one who's going to blacken his name in print.' His response was, 'You must be desperate'. One would have thought he would have praised me for my courage, but he only called me names.

Again, this is not my friend's individual problem. I still consider him a good friend of mine and a moral, upright person. He was only trying to prevent me from getting into serious trouble. This is a perfect example of Chinese paranoia, a fear of trivial things.

Breeding ground for the slave mentality

On my first visit to the United States, I heard about a Chinese in New York who had been mugged and robbed, but refused to identify the culprit after the police caught him. Chinese are paranoid to the point where they don't even know what their legal rights are, or how to assert them. If anything happens to them, the knee-jerk response is 'Forget it'. This 'forgetting it' has caused the death of countless Chinese, and has turned us into a nation of spineless cowards. If I were a foreigner, or better yet a fascist dictator, and *didn't* make it my business to persecute and exploit the Chinese, I would certainly be doing them a great injustice. The psychological environment of neurosis and paranoia I spoke of above is a fertile breeding ground for despots and corrupt bureaucrats, and there is little hope that the particular species of human being that flourishes in this climate will soon die out in China. In traditional Chinese culture, 'acting wisely by playing it safe' is praised time and again, particularly in the great Song dynasty treatise, *A Comprehensive Mirror of Government*. Generations of dictators have rubbed their hands in glee at the thought of the Chinese masses acting wisely by playing it safe, since it makes life very easy for them. This is one reason why the Chinese people continue to degenerate and atrophy.

Chinese civilisation attained the zenith of its glory during the Spring and Autumn and Warring States periods (770–221 BC), after which it began its decline under the influence of Confucian philosophy. By the Eastern Han dynasty (25–220 AD), a law had come into effect stipulating that no educated person could talk about, debate or write anything that trespassed the limits set by his teacher. No one was allowed to challenge what was known as 'the legacy of the master'. Any thought or concept that strayed beyond the confines of this 'legacy' was considered heretical and against the law. As a result, Chinese intellectuals' imaginations were strangled and their ability to reason stunted; it was like sealing up their brains in plastic bags, preventing them from absorbing anything new.

What do I mean when I say that intellectuals lost the ability to reason? Just take a look at all the Chinese newspapers filled with articles by belly-aching columnists. Reasoning is a complex process that operates on several levels at the same time. Sun Kuan-han likes to cite the example of a sphere which is half white and half black. Those who can only see the white side think the entire sphere is white; those who see only the black side think the entire sphere is black. Neither conclusion can be said to be wrong. But looking at both sides of the ball requires imagination and cognitive ability.

An American joke illustrates this point well. A teacher gave his students a barometer and told them 'to use the barometer to measure the height of a building'. Of course the teacher expected the students to do this by calculating the difference between the barometric pressure at the lowest and highest points of the building. But one student came up with a few solutions that had nothing to do with barometric pressure. When he was failed for his work, he complained to the school's administrative committee, 'The teacher asked me to measure the building's height with a barometer, but he didn't specify that I had to do it by measuring barometric pressure. So naturally I used the simplest methods at my disposal. First, I attached the barometer to a string and let it hang down from the roof of the building. Then I measured the length of the string. Secondly, I gave the barometer to the building superintendent in exchange for telling me the height of the building.'

There is nothing devious about either of these methods, unorthodox though they may be. But they reflect the sort of imaginative thinking that drives people with pigeon-hole brains insane.

Here's another tale, called 'The Art of Buying Watermelons'. A shop owner said to one of his clerks, 'Go out, turn west, and when you come to the first bridge, you will see someone selling watermelons. Buy me a four-pound melon.' The clerk went out and headed west, but he couldn't find the bridge or the person selling melons, and returned to the shop empty-handed. The owner swore at him and told him he was a fool. The clerk replied, 'I noticed that they are selling melons in the east'. 'Why didn't you go there and buy them?' 'You didn't tell me to.' Though the owner of the store swore at him for being a fool, he actually regarded the clerk as an ideal employee because of his naivety, obedience and lack of imagination. But had the clerk, noticing that no melons were available in the west, headed east and discovered a heap of sweet melons for sale there, the owner probably would have praised him: 'You're brilliant! You displayed excellent judgement. If only everyone who works here were as smart as you. You're indispensable.' But in fact he would never trust a clerk with such wild imagination. Slaves who think for themselves are dangerous to have around, and should consider themselves lucky if they can stay alive.

Can people raised in a culture that promotes such values think independently? Because Chinese people are incapable of independent thought, they have developed bad taste and poor judgement: they muddle the distinctions between right and wrong; and they have no permanent standards of behaviour. I repeat: we must examine Chinese culture if we want to explain what is wrong with China today.

Developing our judgement

Over the past 4000 years, China has produced only one great thinker: Confucius. In the 2500 years since his death, China's literati have done little more than tack on footnotes to the theories propounded by Confucius and his disciples. Rarely have they contributed anything original to the body of Confucian thought, simply because the traditional culture did not allow it. The minds of the literati were stuck at the bottom of an intellectual stagnant pond, the soy paste vat of Chinese culture. As the contents of this vat grew more and more putrid, the resulting stench was absorbed by the Chinese people. Since the many problems in this opaque, bottomless vat could not be solved by individuals exercising their own reason and intelligence, the literati had to ape other people's way of thinking, or be influenced by other schools of thought. A fresh peach placed in a vat full of putrescent soy paste will soon wither away and turn into a dry turd.

China has its own peculiar way of transforming foreign things and ideas and making them Chinese. You Westerners say you've got democracy; well, we Chinese have democracy too. But in China, *democracy* is understood as follows: you're the *demos* (people), but I've got the *kratos* (power). You Westerners have a legal system; we Chinese have one too. You've got freedom; so do we. Whatever you have, we have too. You've got pedestrian crossing lines painted on the street; we do too, but in China they are there to make it easier for cars to run pedestrians over.

The only way we can do anything about the Ugly Chinaman syndrome is for every individual to cultivate his own personal taste and judgement. One doesn't have to be an accomplished actor to enjoy going to plays. People who don't understand what is happening on stage can at least enjoy the music, the lights, the costumes and the scenery, while those who do understand can appreciate drama as an art form. The ability to make such distinctions is a great achievement in itself.

When I first arrived in Taiwan some thirty years ago, I met a man who owned eight sets of Beethoven's symphonies on records. I asked him if he would sell or give one of them to me, but he refused. Contrary to what I had assumed, each set of the symphonies was performed by a different conductor and orchestra, and they were not at all similar. When I realised that, I felt quite ashamed of myself. This friend was a true connoisseur of music.

During a recent US presidential election, the pre-election debates were broadcast on television in Taiwan. Many people found it remarkable that not once during the debates did either of the candidates reveal anything about their opponent's private lives; American voters disapprove of such tactics, and it would have cost the erring candidate many votes. Chinese politicians are just the opposite. They go out of their way to expose their rivals' personal secrets and perhaps invent a few as well, all couched in the filthiest language.

The quality of the fruit is determined by the quality of the soil in which the tree grows. Similarly, people are the 'fruit' of the societies in which they live. The citizens of a country should cultivate the ability to judge their leaders; otherwise, they only have themselves to blame for the consequences. If we are willing to shout our praises for a man who is unworthy of our respect, who is to blame if he rides roughshod over us? Buying votes is a very disturbing phenomenon. Voters line up to cast their ballots, a man starts handing out money, and the voters ask him, 'Hey, where's my share?'

If this is Chinese political judgement, is China really ready for democracy? Democracy is a privilege to be earned, not a free gift. People say that the Taiwanese Government has relaxed its restrictions on human rights considerably, but I find this a terrifying situation. I have my own freedom and rights, whether the government grants them to me or not. If we had the capacity to make proper judgements, we would demand elections and be rigorous in our selection of candidates. But lacking this capacity, we will never even be able to distinguish a beautiful woman from a pock-marked hag. Who are we to blame for this? If I paint a fake Picasso and you give me half a million bucks for it, who is the fool? You are the one who is blind and entirely lacking in taste and judgement. If there are too many deals like this, no one will buy authentic Picassos, and as the market becomes flooded with fakes, all the real artists will starve to death. Thus, if you buy a fake, you only have yourself to blame. To give another example, you hire a tailor to install a door in your home, and he puts it in upside down. You scold the tailor, 'Are you blind?' But the tailor says, 'Who's blind, you or me? Who told you to hire a tailor to install a lock?' This is a story worth remembering. Without the capacity to make informed judgements, we will always end up making the same mistakes.

Only the Chinese can change themselves

Plagued with so many loathsome qualities, only the Chinese can reform themselves. Foreigners have a duty to help us, not through economic aid but by means of culture. The Chinese ship of state is so large and overloaded that if it sinks many non-Chinese people will perish in the whirlpool as well. I would like to invite all the Americans attending this lecture to extend us a helping hand.

One final point: China is seriously overpopulated. The country has more than a billion hungry mouths to feed, with a collective appetite that could easily devour the Himalayan range. This should remind us that China's problems are complex, and call for a high level of awareness on the part of each and every Chinese. Every one of us must become a discriminating judge and use our ability to examine and appraise ourselves, our friends and our country's leaders. This is our only hope.

Confronting your own ugliness

Interview with the editors of the New York-based Chinese language magazine *China Spring*, conducted in New York City, 12 November 1984

China Spring   Tell us about the problems of being Chinese.

Bo Yang   Chinese history goes back 5000 years. How many of these years can be called good years? Of course we can get emotional about it and boast, 'How wonderful it is to be Chinese, every day is such a happy day!' But if you carefully examine the ancient books that extol the greatness of the Han and Tang dynasties, you will realise that throughout history the Chinese people have suffered constantly. Wars were fought during periods of dynastic succession, and massacres carried out to relieve excess population pressure. Once such crises passed and a degree of stability was restored, the common people fell prey to the depredations of cruel despots and corrupt officials.

CS   This all took place in the past. What about the present situation?

BY   In my youth, I saw with my own eyes at least one aspect of the greatness of the Kuomintang—it was, for a while at least, a political party full of hope and progressive ideas. I come from Hunan, and when the KMT passed through the village I lived in during the Northern Expedition, even the peasants welcomed the KMT troops with open arms. But not long afterwards all that hope evaporated into thin air. Was there any alternative? When the communists took over the mainland in 1949, most of you were very young.

CS   Yes, most of us were born within a few years of 1949.

BY   I was 30 then, so I'm 30 years older than most of you.

CS   When did you leave the mainland?

BY   In 1949, so I've been at this game more than 30 years longer than you have. I was in China during those precious few years when the Chinese Communist Party accomplished great things. Everyone

24

thought the Communist Party was going to save China. But no one imagined how horrible this act of salvation turned out to be. People say the Communist Party only went sour during Mao's later years, but I'm afraid it's not that simple. I've always wondered about the roots of these problems.

CS   Thanks to you, we can hear the Chinese people sobbing.

BY   When I was in Los Angeles a few years ago, someone asked me, 'What do Chinese people have to be proud of?' I answered, 'I'm not at all proud to be Chinese. You tell *me* what Chinese people should be proud of! A powerful country? A great culture? Our contributions to civilisation? Our great music, painting and literature? Is there anything we can really be proud of? Show me something that is uniquely Chinese, something that no other civilisation possesses, or something that we share with another country that we can feel proud about.'

CS   Over the course of the last 5000 years, China has made significant contributions to world civilisation.

BY   Of course it has, but that's all in the past. In the last 500 years, China's contribution has consisted only of dictatorships, corporal punishment, internecine squabbles, and the slave mentality.

CS   Don't many foreigners have great respect for Confucius?

BY   Yes, but there are more Chinese who worship Buddha and Jesus. And some worship Karl Marx and Abraham Lincoln as well.

CS   Can you explain this?

BY   If a foreigner visits Taipei or Beijing once, the Chinese will say that he adores their culture. But how many Chinese people go to the United States and never come back, and once they get a US passport, feel extremely proud of it? Who is worshipping whose culture?

CS   In your opinion, which nation has made the greatest contribution to mankind?

BY   The Anglo-Saxons. First, they developed the parliamentary system of government, probably the most popular and desirable political system in the world. Second, they developed a relatively equitable judicial system based on the jury. All the countries that were formerly colonies of the British Empire chose to adopt the British legal system after they obtained independence. How did England, with its tiny population, manage to rule such a large empire? By the rule of law. This is their greatest contribution to mankind. What has China given to the world over the last 500 years? Some say a sense of morality and honesty. Are the Chinese people moral and honest? Yes they are, but only on paper. The characteristics that distinguish Chinese people today are uncouthness, insincerity and narrow-mindedness.

CS   An old saying goes, 'Don't assume the worst about other people'. But this is precisely the way most people think. We should take a good look at ourselves, and try to understand our own problems before we start worrying about others.

BY The worst habit the Chinese have is the way they apply high standards to other people, but not to themselves.

CS This is basically a cultural problem.

BY That's right. Some of you are from mainland China. You're critical of the communists, so you start a democracy movement. My guess is that you are not doing this out of selfish motives. If you were acting solely out of self interest, you could just as well go back to China and find a well-paying job, especially those of you with graduate degrees. The people in Taiwan who are campaigning for greater human rights, improvements in the legal system, and more freedom and democracy share your ideals.

I joined the KMT when I was eighteen years old. If I had been a good boy and stayed out of trouble all those years, I would at least be a petty bureaucrat by now. But because I believed in those ideals, I never became a petty bureaucrat and landed myself in prison. The question is, why do we continue to pursue these ideals, but never realise them? We want to reform the political system, but if we fail, do we have any other choices? The only solution is revolution. If the revolution fails, you lose your head. If it succeeds, you'll end up ruling the roost like the last bunch of despots.

CS You consider yourself a member of the KMT, but the KMT kicked you out a long time ago.

BY One's thinking develops as one grows older. At the beginning of the Anti-Japanese War (1937–1945), I was in officer training school. We were young then, we cared only about saving China from the Japanese, and we had very little awareness of party politics. If China were defeated, how could there be any political parties in the first place? The idea, popular at the time, of a 'party-state' under the KMT was an absurdity. I had always been loyal to Chiang Kai-shek. But when China started falling apart, I had a personal crisis. What was happening was beyond Chiang's control, I thought. And of course he only wanted the best for China. It was the same with Mao Zedong. Didn't Mao have the best interests of China at heart? How did these two great men let the situation in China get out of hand? The problem lay deeper. Chinese culture was to blame.

CS Have you delved into this question in depth?

BY I've started to. Nowadays, if you listen to the Chinese Government, they say, whatever the United States has, China has too. The US has a constitution, so does China. But the Chinese constitution is a bit like a theatre marquee; it changes every time there's a new star. Why bother having a constitution in the first place? And how do you get people to trust it? This has a lot to do with culture.

There's an old Chinese saying: when you transplant tangerines from one bank of the Huai River to the other, they turn out bitter and thick-skinned. Chinese culture is like the soil on the other side of the Huai River. For example, if you plant an American apple tree in China, the fruit will turn out to be like hard turds. The soy sauce vat spoils everything that goes into it. By studying in the United States you can get a good understanding of American culture and the American political system. But when you go back to China, whatever you've learned is bound to be drowned in the sauce.

CS You compare Chinese culture to a soy sauce vat. Sun Kuan-han has also criticised the soy sauce vat of Chinese culture in his books. When you talk about this soy sauce vat culture, do you mean the inherent flaws in the Chinese character?

BY I should start out by saying that I am not an academic, so I may not be able to provide you with the sort of clear definitions you want. For a long time I've wanted to write a book called *The Ugly Chinaman* but I never had the time to do it. I learned a lot from reading *The Ugly American* and *The Ugly Japanese*. Those two books are filled with observations and self-criticism that reflect the authors' view of the darker side of life in America and Japan; they can hardly be called scholarly analyses. I've heard experts talking about various countries' problems, but they use too many technical terms and too much jargon. I want to make one general statement: Chinese people are not inherently bad, or inherently inferior to others. In American schools, many Chinese score the highest marks, which proves that they have high IQs. But a Chinese person with a high IQ will only perform well by himself. If three Chinese people with high IQs get together, they cancel each other out. This is one of the deficiencies in Chinese culture I have been talking about. The soy sauce vat can lower people's IQs.

How this vat came into being is not an important issue, and I am still not clear about how it happened. My feeling is that it grew out of Confucian thought. About a hundred years after it became the official ideology in China (in the Eastern Han dynasty, 25–220 AD), Confucianism became dogmatic and was plagued by formulas. In those days, an educated person was forbidden to think, teach or discuss anything in variance with what *they* had been taught. Students and scholars spent their lives parroting whatever their teachers had taught them. If you crossed the invisible line of orthodoxy and said too much, it did you no good, and actually constituted a crime. In the Han dynasty such offences were not considered serious. But during the Ming (1368–1644) and Qing (1644–1911) dynasties, when the authorities declared that everything had to be explained according to Zhu Xi's (1130–1200) philosophy, it was forbidden to cite Wang Yangming (1472–1529). Scholars were not permitted to think independently, because everything had already been thought out for them. Thus they became uncreative and unimaginative, and were incapable of making critical judgements.

CS During the Third Reich, Hitler said, 'You don't have to think about anything. Der Führer has everything worked out for you.' Today in China the Communist Party makes all the decisions, since of course they know better than everybody else.

BY That's fascism, feudalism and obscurantism all rolled into one. Every feudal despot thinks he's smarter than everyone else. Slaves who can think for themselves are a threat to the state. No feudal dictator can tolerate the existence of thinking people.

CS Throughout Chinese history, many emperors made a point of keeping the Chinese people under a veil of ignorance.

BY But the ability to think for oneself and give free rein to one's imagination are preconditions for creativity and inventiveness. If you deprive people of the right to think, they even lose the ability to imitate others. Something as simple as parroting others requires a certain amount of creativity.

CS Can we hold Chinese culture accountable for the particular quality which we call 'Chineseness', or is 'Chineseness' responsible for the formation of Chinese culture? Or are they simply two sides of the same coin?

BY That's the same as asking: which came first, the chicken or the egg?

CS I've always assumed that Chinese culture and Chineseness were one and the same thing. I would like to raise three questions:

1 What are the main weaknesses of Chinese culture and Chineseness?
2 What are the causes of these weaknesses?
3 What is the relationship between the deficiencies in the Chinese national character and the fact that China has never developed a democratic political system? And is there anything we can do to change this situation?

I think the absence of an understanding of the concept of law is something particular to the Chinese. Here is an example of this attitude. A friend of mine from Taiwan who was studying in the United States told me about how he had taken his father, who had come from Taiwan to visit him, for a ride in his car. They were driving at night, and when my friend stopped the car at a red light, his father said to him, 'Why do you have to wait for the green light? There aren't any other cars or people around.'

Americans almost always obey red lights, but Chinese people will ask, 'Why does it matter if you go through a red light?' Chinese people don't understand the abstract concept of law. A few minutes ago you said how difficult it was for Chinese people to co-operate, even if everyone concerned is extremely intelligent. This is a serious problem too.

BY   Going back to the question of Chinese culture and Chineseness, culture sometimes develops in irrational ways, like those toy robots that head off in the opposite direction when they run into an obstacle. It's the same as pushing a boulder down a mountain. It might take a lot of strength to get it rolling, but once it starts moving, there's no way to stop it.

CS   That's what happened during the Cultural Revolution.

BY   They called it the 'Great Proletarian Cultural Revolution', but it was more like one vast Chinese family feud. If Chinese people don't solve the problem of bickering among themselves that lies at the heart of the Cultural Revolution, China will never become a powerful nation, and the Chinese people will never be happy. For 5000 years, Chinese people have failed to realise the benefits of being broadminded.

CS   Chinese people have always given the impression of being conceited and arrogant.

BY   The Chinese mind is extremely complex. Not only do politicians stick to their own point of view once a consensus has been reached; when three hooligans in the same gang get together, they soon end up in a brawl. This sort of intolerance for others' opinions is despicable.

CS   When Fritz Mondale realised that he had lost the presidential election to Ronald Reagan, he made a public announcement: 'Ronald Reagan is our new president'. You can only find magnanimity like that in democratic countries like the USA.

BY   Chinese people are overly concerned about losing face, so they never surrender or admit to making mistakes. To err is human; only animals are perfect. When a Chinese person fails at something, all he can do is curse and shout. It will take another 300 years before Chinese officials start acting like Fritz Mondale.

CS   The only thing Chinese leaders excel at is engaging in power struggles.

BY   Power corrupts, but it also turns people into ignorant pigs. Do the feudalistic fascist dictators of China really believe that all that kowtowing and shouting of 'Long live so-and-so' is any more useful than a mosquito buzzing in their ears? Actually it's all a pack of lies. Absolute power damages the central nervous system and turns people into dimwits.

CS   Perhaps Chinese people are addicted to politics and can't give it up?

BY Chinese people like to talk politics, that's for sure, but they shy away from actual engagement. This is a kind of paranoia, a totally unfounded fear. Most people muddle their way through life and never exercise their own legitimate rights or know how to make use of the power they have. They will only act to change their own situation if someone with greater authority than themselves relinquishes a bit of authority to them.

CS Chinese people's ignorance of their own rights and powers is a serious problem. In China, the communists subjected countless people to mind-bending 'struggle' sessions and threw them in jail. Then a new ruler took over and these suffering victims were released and 'rehabilitated'. Having gained their 'freedom', some of them went out of their way to thank the Communist Party for acting so kindly on their behalf.

At a conference in Los Angeles, a visiting scholar who had been persecuted as a rightist in China told us: 'The party rehabilitated me and let me go abroad to do research. Could they possibly treat me better than that?' What can you say to someone like that? It would never occur to him that going overseas is the right of every citizen. How pathetic it is that he can only perceive coming to the United States to do research as a blessing conferred upon him by the grace of the Chinese Communist Party.

BY Once a slave, always a slave. People like that can't help themselves. A lot of Chinese people who become American citizens never vote. It doesn't occur to them that voting is the only effective means at their disposal of protecting their own interests. The son of a Chinese friend of mine who lives in Iowa was bitten by a neighbour's dog. The dog's owner was known in his neighbourhood for being nasty, so my friend thought that because his son was not seriously injured, it was just as well to forget about the incident. When the boy's school teacher heard about what had happened, he told the boy that his father was wrong, and encouraged him by saying that Chinese–Americans should not give people the impression they can be bullied about. Finally he suggested that they go to the police. As a result, the dog's owner was fined and forced to make a public apology. This is a question of power, not money. Chinese people think that forbearance is a virtue. Actually, passivity in the face of injustice comes from being insulted so often that one becomes numb to it. But by praising this deficiency as 'forbearance' Chinese people can put their consciences at ease. Few Chinese are willing to fight for their own rights.

CS Please explain why.

BY They're neurotic and paranoid. They're afraid they'll lose in the end.

CS Aren't such people being dishonest with themselves?

BY Chinese people have a natural gift for bragging, exaggerating, telling lies, and slandering other people. There's something I've always wondered about. America is full of psychiatrists, but you will have a hard time finding one in China. The reason for this is, when you see a head shrinker, you're supposed to tell the truth. Chinese people *never* tell the truth. If they've got a pain in their buttocks, they tell the doctor they've got an earache. If a woman doesn't like a particular man, she'll tell the psychiatrist the man doesn't like her. How can the doctor do a proper job if his patients always tell lies?

CS There's an old Chinese joke about a warlord who gave a banquet. One of his guests brought him a basketful of bananas for a gift, but because the warlord had never eaten a banana before, he popped it in his mouth without peeling it. In order not to make him lose face, all the other guests ate their bananas the same way.

BY That's old-fashioned face-saving. If one of your modern-day dictator types did that, they'd come up with some profound philosophical explanation for the benefits of eating banana peels.

CS Didn't Lin Biao once say, 'You can't accomplish anything great unless you lie'?

BY That sort of thinking has a terribly corrupting influence on people. To praise lying as if it were something glorious!

CS An old saying goes: 'If the ruler deceives the people, the people will deceive the ruler'. Dishonesty is something mutual.

BY There's a question of retribution here. If one person deceives another, there's no great harm done. But if a feudal despot rules his country through deception, the entire population may turn against him.

CS Chinese people are concerned with human relationships and what they call 'human feelings', and think that Americans lack such feelings.

BY Chinese people only act in an open and human way with their friends. With strangers they can be cold and cruel, and start swearing as soon as a disagreement arises. A Chinese woman author who lives in Iowa received a threatening letter in Chinese in the mail. She translated it into English and showed it to her American secretary, who became very upset. And when the author's American husband read it, he telephoned the FBI. Translated literally, the passage they found so disturbing was: 'Hope you suffer the result. Wish you having no burial place for your body when you die.' Actually, this is nothing more than toilet graffiti. Chinese people talk like this so often it's second nature to them.

CS In the Chinese countryside, there are people who do nothing but 'curse the street'—walk through the village insulting people left and right. During the Cultural Revolution, when people accused of being 'bad elements' were forced to beat a cymbal and criticise themselves in public, some of them went around shouting, 'I'm a goddamned counter-revolutionary, I'm a stinking bad element!'

BY Being forced to insult yourself—remember how the character Phoenix taught her maid to slap herself in the face in the novel *The Dream of the Red Chamber*—is both humiliating and cruel. If a person, or a whole nation, lacks a sense of self-esteem, what sort of a person or country can they be? No better than a bunch of wild animals!

CS Chinese people love to brag and boast. If a man goes fishing and doesn't catch anything, he'll buy two fish at the market so he can show everyone what he's caught. Of course the two fish will be exactly the same size.

BY In Iowa I met some writers from East Germany and Bulgaria. What I liked most about them was the way they talked straight off the shoulder.

CS Many Chinese people in the US think that Americans are stupid, naive and easily taken advantage of. Actually this statement says more about the Chinese than the Americans.

BY This is pettiness and ignorance. Chinese people think that being good to others is stupid. Actually, Chinese people who think this way make China the human jungle it is today. I feel ashamed whenever I think about such things.

CS Since Chinese who think like that have nothing good inside them to begin with, they can only imagine that everyone else in the world is selfish.

BY A Chinese man I met in Iowa opened a big restaurant. The Americans who know him say he's a hardworking businessman, but the other Chinese in the area are insanely jealous of him. Once during a lecture, someone called me anti-Chinese and pro-Western. But how many Chinese people do you know that aren't 'pro-Western'? Why don't Chinese men wear their hair in a queue like they did in the Qing dynasty? And why don't women bind their feet? People also say I insult my own ancestors. Actually I talk straight and tell the truth because I do have great respect for my ancestors.

CS Why do some people think this way?

BY Again, it is part of the legacy of feudal thinking. Both the Chinese Communist Party and the Kuomintang were heavily influenced by the Soviet Union. The Soviet Union in turn was influenced by the Russian Orthodox church, which like the Roman Catholic Church practises confession. The communists simply turned voluntary confession into forced confession and compulsory self-criticism. Combine this with Oriental poverty and backwardness and you end up with a powerful force for repression.

CS In the late 1950s, the Chinese Communist Party asked 'bourgeois elements' and members of the democratic parties to 'make a clean breast of themselves' and join the proletariat in the so-called 'loyalty and honesty movement'. In those days, most people trusted the communists, and willingly confessed indiscretions they had committed in word, thought or action. The communists tried to be fair and open about this: 'Let bygones be bygones', they said, and accordingly promised that anyone who told the truth would be let off with no further trouble. But before long the communists had to eat their Marxist hat. All of these confessions were recorded in personal dossiers, which are kept in the personnel department of every work unit, ready to be used against that person when necessary. And sure enough, when the Cultural Revolution rolled around, the material in the dossiers was brought out as evidence in the 'struggle' sessions. This taught people a lesson: never tell the truth; lie to protect yourself.

There's a joke about this. During the Cultural Revolution, when people were being forced to write 'self-criticisms', a few clever people hung out shingles that read: 'We ghost-write self-criticisms. Standard self-criticism—50 cents; penetrating self-criticism—$1.'

Writing a self-criticism entailed going against the dictates of one's own conscience, deceiving oneself and deceiving one's superiors. Ghost-writing self-criticisms was akin to ghost-writing lies. It became a business, with its own scale of prices. Small lies were cheap, big lies cost more.

BY It's amazing that lying was considered a virtue and became a kind of business. Was this ghost-writing of self-confessions taking place in the cities or the countryside?

CS Both. Some parents had their children write their confessions for them.

BY And the Communist Party did nothing about it?

CS Of course not. Party members had other people write confessions for them too. They followed a formula: first you listed your 'problems', or mistakes, and then you 'sublimated' them ideologically to the plane of class struggle and line struggle.

BY What's that all about?

CS For example, if I did something trivial like take your pen, I could be accused of being a corrupt member of the bourgeois, and a class enemy. Later I would be exploited by other class enemies, and in working for their benefit would eventually cause the death of thousands. The line struggle involves contradictions between the capitalist and socialist line. There's also the question of investigating your background. Everyone's got a 'thought background', 'family background' and 'class background', which is traced back three generations. Your superiors will only accept your self-criticism when they see you grovelling in self-hate. Even Deng Xiaoping went through this many times; he wrote two self-criticisms for Hua Guofeng. This ruse eventually became a tool for political manipulation. Of course it's pure fabrication. People were just telling each other lies.

BY   Did it accomplish anything except turn everybody in China into immoral creatures?

CS   When the class and line struggle was carried out, the evidence went into people's dossiers. The communists are fastidious dialecticians. Whenever they want to attack you, they select from your dossier whatever evidence they need. This is actually a highly sophisticated way of running a country. In the 30-odd years they have been ruling China, the communists have developed all the vile characteristics of the Chinese people and raised them to an impressively high level.

BY   People ask me, did the Cultural Revolution put an end to all the bad tendencies in Chinese culture? I think it actually reinforced them.

CS   You can be sure that in China whatever the Communist Party opposes or criticises will eventually flourish. To give one example, when they criticised the writer Bai Hua, more people read his works. A country's political system and the character of its people are closely linked. Under a corrupt political system, all the bad elements in that culture will thrive. And this will only reinforce the political system, no matter how bad it is.

BY   When I was a boy they told us the story of how George Washington had chopped down a cherry tree, as a way of teaching us to be honest. But if George's father had whipped him every time he told the truth, young George wouldn't have remained honest for long.

CS   Why are Chinese so unaware of the backwardness of their own culture? Some people think that because China is so poor, and because so few people get enough to eat or have enough to wear, it's acceptable for Chinese people to act immorally. There is an old saying, 'The rich should not squander their wealth, the poor should not be demoralised'.

BY   That's very idealistic. Few people can actually live up to that.

CS   What are the positive aspects of Chinese culture?

BY   The Chinese value friendship more than people in the West. Westerners prefer to do things on their own rather than together with other people. I prefer the Chinese way. In Chinese society, people need friends. There is an old saying: 'At home rely on your father and mother, in society rely on your friends'. At home your parents will protect you; outside, you can only depend on your friends. In the West, people don't need their friends to protect them, the government takes care of that. Friendship in the West has an entirely different connotation.

For example, in the USA, if your car breaks down, a total stranger will stop and help you. Few Chinese would do that, unless they knew you. A friend of mine in Iowa was driving on a snowy day and his car slipped off the road into a ditch. Two Black men stopped and spent the next three hours helping my friend haul his car back onto the road. My friend wanted to thank them in some way, but when he asked them their names, one of them said, 'If I was in this situation, wouldn't you stop and help me too?'. My friend never forgot that. Genuine kindness is the sort of kindness that takes place between perfect strangers. It has no gradations and bears no relation to how well the people involved know each other.

CS The Bible says that you should love your enemies. Chinese people only care about their friends. Americans don't seem to set so much store by human relationships, but when you really need help they will always be there. Perhaps the Bible has something to do with this.

BY I like the way Americans say 'hello' to strangers. When Chinese run into people they don't know, all they do is trade dirty looks.

CS Generally speaking, Western people don't seem to be very patriotic. But they certainly can be when the need arises.

BY On the other hand, Chinese people go overboard with their patriotism, to the point where even the most trivial act is a matter of patriotism. As a result of 'loving their country' so much, they have literally loved China to death. They ought to stop loving China so much. China doesn't need that much love. Or if Chinese have some energy left over, they ought to spend it loving themselves, making themselves better people. True patriotism begins with loving and respecting yourself.

CS Someone once said that Chinese can be proud of the fact that Chinese scientists have developed atomic bombs and hydrogen bombs.

BY The only thing worth being proud of is increasing the happiness of the Chinese people by making some improvement in the quality of life in China. What's better: a billion beggars with solid gold begging bowls, or a population that is well-clothed, well-fed and well-educated?

CS In places like Gansu, on the high loess plains of Central Asia, the people are terribly poor. Water there is a real problem. Every family digs a hole in the ground, and collects water in it only when it rains or snows. They use this water for washing, drinking, and feeding their pigs. Every drop is precious.

BY I am disturbed that the Chinese seem to be unable to create a modern nation for themselves.

CS Mao Zedong made many mistakes. The Kuomintang and the Chinese Communist Party also made a lot of mistakes. But they're all Chinese, all products of the Middle Kingdom. Could they survive very long anywhere else but in China? Of course, Americans have their own problems.

BY I don't think the Chinese people are quite ready to handle the sort of problems one finds in the US. A Chinese professor teaching in the US gave a lecture in Beijing recently in which he said, 'The American presidential elections are as simple as a children's game'. This is not only ignorance, it's shameless. The way Liu Shaoqi, the former Chinese president, was locked up and left to die in a jail in Kaifeng is a child's game. People say that Americans waste a lot of money. But wasting money is certainly preferable to wasting human lives. Some people simply don't know where the real problems lie and need others to point out the truth to them.

At home my wife plays the role of sheriff, constantly reminding me to keep my big mouth shut. When Jesus was nailed to the cross, he said, 'Forgive them, for they know not what they do'. When I was young, I thought this was a lot of rubbish. Later I came to realise that this made some sense, but I remained suspicious. Now that I'm an old man, I can understand the profundity of Jesus' statement. The Red Guards, for example, thought they were doing the right thing, and didn't know how much destruction they were causing. Given the way things happen in China, I feel that certain topics are best broached outside of China, and then allowed to filter back in. Of course when I started doing this, a lot of people found it intolerable. Specifically, when I gave my speech on 'The Ugly Chinaman' at Iowa University, someone told me that everything I said was wrong because I hadn't read a certain book. You see, it's hard for Chinese people to get to the crux of a problem. They'd rather smooth things over and pretend the problem doesn't exist.

CS How can we improve ourselves?

BY For years I've been saying that the Chinese people in Taiwan are uncivilised bores, but when I discovered that Chinese people on the mainland are even less civilised I became very depressed. Let's start with language. Chinese people are constantly telling each other to say things like 'thank you', 'excuse me', and 'may I help you'. At the same time, every Chinatown I've been to is a filthy mess. Compared to Little Italy and Little Tokyo, for example, Chinatown is a pigsty. Before Chinese people start talking about politeness, they ought to clean up their own neighbourhoods.

CS What do you have to say about the future of China and the Chinese people?

BY This future of China depends on the level of awareness of the average Chinese in the street. Can he or she identify our shortcomings? This is a matter of culture and education, not politics.

CS If we want to institute democracy in China, the first step is to transform our national character. That means escaping from the soy sauce vat once and for all. If the majority of Chinese lack basic self-awareness, it will be impossible for China to make any progress. At present very few people in China realise the degree to which they are enslaved; and the few that do understand are powerless to do anything about it.

BY Everyone should know that the purpose of a political party is to serve the state, not vice-versa, and that the relationship between the people and the government is one of authority and obligations.

CS The Chinese Communist Party used to boast: Heaven is great, earth is great, but nothing is as great as the loving kindness of the Party; even motherly love is nothing compared to Chairman Mao's love for the people'. Now in China they're pushing the 'five carefuls, four beautifuls and three loves'. One of the things you're supposed to 'love' is the Chinese Communist Party.

BY That's pure idealism and fascist obscurantism. The truth is, the government cannot fool the people for long, and in the end the people will turn around and put one over on the government. The way the communists run China, they're only fooling themselves. I don't think this situation will last forever in China.

CS Political systems, national character, and basic human nature are all mutually dependent. Changing the Chinese national character is going to take a long time, but we don't have to wait that long to establish a democratic political system. Actually, democracy is a key factor in reforming national character.

BY We must try to change China now, as well as over the next millennium. We can have a thousand-year plan, but we should be satisfied with any progress we make today. Once the momentum starts, it will be hard to stop. What matters is whether our efforts make the emergence of democracy inevitable.

CS Chinese people are an intelligent bunch, that's for sure. But too many Chinese are merely shrewd and self-protective; they lack wisdom and foresight. Americans may appear dumb and naive on the surface, but this can conceal great wisdom. In the long run, wisdom is superior to shrewdness.

BY Chinese people are so clever, they think everyone else in the world is an idiot. If a Chinese falls out of an 80-storey building by accident, when he sails by the 50th floor and notices a couple drinking coffee inside, he'll find the time to ridicule them for not knowing that they will choke to death on their coffee before finishing their cups.

The Chinese and the soy paste vat

Speech given at Confucius Plaza in
Chinatown, New York, 16 August 1981.
Transcribed and edited by the *Beimei Daily*,
New York

The theme I have been asked to talk about today is 'The Chinese and the Soy Paste Vat'.

Let us begin with a story. A man once asked a Buddhist monk—everyone knows that Buddhists believe in *karma*—who had attained enlightenment: 'Can you tell me what sort of person I was in my former life? And what sort of person will I be in my next life?' The monk responded with the following verse:

> If you wish to know your former life,
> Your present life embodies it.
> If you wish to know your future life,
> Your present life creates it.

According to the theory of *karma*, if you are a happy person, you must have been generally honest and generous to others in your previous life. If your life is full of suffering, then in your last life you must have done many evil things. This story contains an important message. If you are a Buddhist, of course it will make sense to you. But if you don't believe in *karma*, then perhaps you will perceive some other significance in it.

I tell this tale because in some way it is related to Chinese culture. Most of you in the audience are Chinese. By Chinese I mean that you have Chinese blood, no matter what nationality you are. You will always be Chinese, whether you like it or not, and there is nothing that anyone can do to change that. 'Chinese' here means 'Chinese' in the broader sense; this is a question of genes, not geography.

For the last 200 years, all Chinese people have shared the common hope that China can develop into a strong nation, and that the Chinese

38

people can become the greatest nation on earth. But for a long time, we have been weak, and the object of foreigners' contempt and scorn. Why? Of course this is our own responsibility. But we can ask the same question from the cultural point of view, referring back to the story I just told about *karma*: Why is China such a feeble, backward nation, and why are Chinese people's lives so full of suffering? In China, everyone, both rich and poor, weak and strong, shares the same aspirations for their country, as well as the same pessimism about it.

When I was a boy in school, one of my teachers told us: 'China's hopes rest on you'. And now it's our turn to tell the younger generation: 'You're the hope for China's future'. How many more generations will say the same thing? Chinese people in the West feel this unfulfilled longing in a more acute way than Chinese people in China; and they also have greater expectations. In addition to our own inability to shoulder responsibility for the despicable level to which life in China has sunk today, we must also bear the onerous burden that traditional Chinese culture has bequeathed us. We might call this phenomenon 'cultural *karma*'.

In the Boston Museum the other day I saw a pair of tiny Chinese shoes made especially for women with bound feet, the sort of shoes my grandmother might have worn. Many women of my generation had no choice but to bind their feet when they were girls. I know that young people will find the whole business of foot-binding hard to imagine. Why did the Chinese people invent a practice as cruel as foot-binding, and force it on one half of the Chinese population over the course of a thousand years? Foot-binding entailed breaking the bones of the foot and allowing the flesh to rot, thus preventing women from walking in a normal manner. For a thousand years, why didn't anyone stand up and declare that there was something unnatural or unhealthy about foot-binding, instead of praising distorted feet as something beautiful?

Chinese culture didn't leave the men unscathed either. There were eunuchs in China since ancient times. In fact, before the Song dynasty, wealthy people could castrate their servants with impunity. This horrific practice was finally outlawed in the eleventh century.

These are just two of the many irrational and inhumane aspects of Chinese culture. And over the course of our long history, many unspeakable practices nearly got out of hand.

Every culture flows on unceasingly like a great river. But as the centuries go by, cultures accumulate all sorts of flotsam and jetsam, such as dead fish, dead cats, and dead rats. When this detritus piles up on the river bed, the river ceases to flow and turns stagnant. The deeper the river, the thicker the layer of sludge; the older the river, the more thoroughly the sludge rots, until the river turns into one huge fermentation vat, a stinking repository of everything filthy and disgusting under the sun.

First I should explain the soy paste vat. When I grew up in North China, there were fermentation vats used for making bean sauce in every home, though I never could figure out what material they were made out of. But if you have ever eaten Peking duck, you've had the sauce: a thick paste made primarily out of soy beans and wheat flour. It's as viscous as mud, and doesn't flow, the very opposite of the surging waves of the Yellow River. Because the paste remains in the vat untouched and unstirred, and because the water content is constantly evaporating, the paste grows thicker and thicker as time goes by. Chinese culture, what we can call the *karma* of Chineseness, undergoes a similar process.

The soy paste vat is a perfect metaphor for the traditional Chinese bureaucracy. In the past, an education was the only key that could open the door to the world of officialdom. The invisible and impalpable Chinese 'bureaucracy'—there is no proper equivalent in English—was an outgrowth of the imperial examination system. Once a person entered the ranks of officialdom, he automatically cut himself off from the common people and became their enemy. In traditional China, educated people had one and only one goal in life: to become officials. The old saying, 'In books one can find faces as fine as jade and golden mansions' means that if you became an official you can have all the women and money you wish. Although the saying 'Every craft and trade has its own unrivalled master' confers a certain amount of respect on accomplished individuals in every field, anyone who was not from the literati class was despised, like a blue-collar labourer. The literati had their own distinct dress that people from other classes were not permitted to wear, and their own special sedan chairs to ride around in. Everything in Chinese feudal society revolved around the interests of the literati. Over the centuries, the system that fostered these nefarious social distinctions had a profound influence on Chinese society. The Chinese economy remained static, while in the area of political culture China remained stuck at the bottom of the soy paste vat. One distinguishing characteristic of this culture was the way the bureaucracy set the standards for the entire society, and ran the country for their own personal benefit. In modern times, this took the form of Mao's doctrine of 'putting politics in command'. As a result, the soy paste of Chinese culture became thicker and more like mud.

Centuries of steeping in the soy paste vat has made Chinese people selfish, egotistical and jealous of others. Though I have only been in the United States for a few weeks, my first impression is that Americans are friendly and happy people; they seem to be smiling all the time. When I visit Chinese people in their homes here, I notice that the children seem happy enough, but that the adults hardly smile at all. Perhaps Chinese people have different facial muscles from Americans? Or maybe Chinese people are glum by nature.

Few Chinese people have asked themselves whether they *themselves* are responsible for the fact that the Chinese national character—what I call Chineseness—is entirely lacking in youthful vitality. Chinese people are always fighting among themselves, and find it very difficult to co-operate with each other. There is a story about a sergeant in the Japanese police who trained his cadets by telling them to suspect that everyone they set eyes on is a thief. This is fine for cops, but Chinese people always think somebody is trying to take advantage of them. It is this constant suspicion of other people's motives that has made Chinese people as spineless as 'a bowl of sand', to borrow a phrase from Sun Yat-sen.

China has huge reserves of natural resources and a vast population. If the one-billion-plus Chinese population could someday get their act together, they could easily surpass the Japanese, not to mention every other nation in Asia.

The pernicious influence of thousands of years of feudal and authoritarian government which has kept the Chinese people pickling away in the soy paste vat has crippled our thinking, hampered our judgement, perverted our world view, and kept us bottled up inside a set of thick walls. This influence has also impaired our ability to make moral judgments and deprived us of the courage to act on principle. As a result, we can only react to the world through our emotions and our intuition. In sum, we have lost the ability to think straight. All our values, be they moral or political, come out of this bean paste vat, where there is no such thing as right and wrong, and where nothing is ever black and white. Relativity reigns supreme, and only rarely do people analyse issues carefully. Centuries of going around in circles in precisely the same rut culminated in an event that defies explanation in terms of historical *karma*: the Opium Wars of the 1840s.

The violent blow European culture struck at China during the Opium Wars taught the Chinese a wonderful lesson in 'national shame'. It was indeed a rude awakening. The Japanese respond to historical events quite differently from the Chinese. When the United States Navy sank two Japanese ships back in the eighteenth century, the Japanese responded by opening their doors to the West. The Japanese realised the advantages of doing this; for them, shame acts as a form of inspiration.

Maybe we Chinese should be grateful for the Opium Wars. Where would China be today without them? Some of the men in the audience today would be wearing their hair in a Manchu-style queue, and many of the ladies would have bound feet. You'd also wear long gowns and riding jackets, and take a sedan chair or sampan to work. If the Opium Wars had taken place 300 years earlier than they did, China might have had a head start on modernisation, and if they had taken place 1000 years ago, Chinese history would be unimaginably different. I feel that this lesson in national shame constituted a major frontal attack on the culture of the soy paste vat. Without the Opium Wars, Chinese people would still be rotting away in that vat, that is, if they hadn't first suffocated or drowned.

The violent intrusion of Western culture during the Opium Wars suggests that the Qing dynasty was the greatest period in Chinese history. Had the wars taken place in the Ming dynasty, China would never have survived the onslaught. In retrospect, we can say that the sooner modern Western civilisation appeared in ancient Cathay, the better. That striking confrontation with the West presented China with a profound historical and cultural challenge, and left behind the modern material and spiritual components of Western civilisation.

All of that—airplanes, artillery, automobiles and subway trains— showed the Chinese people how different the rest of the world was, and gave us an entirely new appreciation of material culture. Western politics and scholarship opened up new realms of awareness for us, as concepts like democracy, freedom, the rights of man and the rule of law were transplanted onto Chinese soil.

There's an old saying: 'Human destiny depends on Heaven'. Actually, human destiny depends on who you are. If I murder someone, my destiny *would* depend on Heaven. But if a powerful and influential person kills someone, well, what's one human life worth anyway?

Another old saying goes: 'Cherish the people, not the ruler'. This is pure idealism, something that has never taken place in China. Throughout China's long history, dynasties rose and fell, but the dynastic system itself never changed. The difference between one dynasty and the next only became apparent when the new dynasty burnt down the imperial palaces of the old, and constructed new palaces in their place, just to prove how different they were. To justify such destruction they claimed that the former rulers were tyrants, while they themselves were benevolent; it was only natural for benevolent rulers to destroy tyrants' palaces. As one dynasty succeeded the next, there was no evolution in political thought and there were no new ideas; just more palace-burning. This also explains why there are so few ancient buildings in China.

Some of the more admirable elements of Chinese political thought bear similarities to Western concepts, such as the notion that 'the ruler will be punished like his subjects', but in China carrying this out is little more than a fantastic daydream. If an emperor and a commoner commit an identical crime, the two of them will not be accused of the same crime. There was no democracy, freedom or rule of law in China. Some experts have claimed that people in China were free to curse the emperor, but this 'freedom' was severely restricted, and controlled very carefully by the emperors themselves. If someone wanted to curse the emperor, he had to do it secretly, behind the emperor's back. Freedom was strictly limited. Of course you were free to think whatever you wished, but democracy and the rule of law were unknown.

To acquire all the good things in life requires a struggle, unlike in the Garden of Eden, where God did all the hard work. Because of their long sojourn in the soy paste vat, Chinese people have developed a strong tendency towards resignation. On the one hand, they like to brag and exaggerate, on the other they're self-indulgent and self-pitying. I once saw a film about a woman with a split personality: one part of her was beautiful, rich and respectable; the other side was dissolute, shameless and obscene. She couldn't integrate the two, but when her psychiatrist made it possible for her to confront her predicament, she committed suicide. When we examine our own weaknesses, do we dare to face reality, and approach our faults rationally?

We Chinese ought to learn to 'know ourselves'. Chinese people have little experience with rational introspection; our self-images rest on our emotions. For example, a husband says to his wife, 'You're not good to me', so she throws her food on the dining table and says to him, 'How am I not good to you? If I'm so bad to you, why do I bother cooking dinner for you?' This is pure nastiness on her part. Having no understanding at all is better than having this sort of understanding.

The influence of Western culture in China brought about definite changes in Chinese political thought as well as in the realm of morality. In the past husbands beat their wives as a matter of course, but try getting away with that these days! It's a blessing for young people today that some of the more backward aspects of traditional Chinese culture have fallen by the wayside. There has also been significant progress in art, poetry, fiction, drama and dance.

Every time I bring up the subject of Western civilisation and culture, someone always accuses me of being a xenophiliac, a person who loves to bootlick foreigners. But what's wrong with being a xenophiliac? Foreigners generally behave in a more civilised manner than Chinese people, and their 'guns' work a lot better than our 'bows and arrows'. If your friend is a better scholar than you are or has higher standards of morality, what's so bad about having respect for him? Chinese people are too cowardly to express praise for other people, but they have plenty of courage when it comes to lashing out at others. The overpowering influence of the soy paste vat culture turns Chinese people into 'bitter oranges'. Tangerines taste sweet and delicious if they are planted in the proper soil. But if you plant a tangerine tree where the soil and climate is poor, it will only produce small, inedible fruit. Sun Kuan-han, who worked on my behalf during the ten years I was in jail, planted cabbage seeds from Shandong province in Pittsburgh, Pennsylvania. But the cabbage that grew there was nothing like the original plant.

The Japanese are marvellous imitators. They can take anything and reproduce it in such a way that the copy is impossible to distinguish from the original. Chinese people are incompetent when it comes to this sort of thing. The ability to imitate confers great benefits upon the Japanese because it enables them to study selectively the outstanding aspects of other cultures. Chinese people love to justify their own weaknesses by mouthing such lame excuses as 'It doesn't have Chinese national characteristics'. During the Sino–Japanese War of 1895, a number of Japanese generals were watching the Chinese navy carry out some military exercises. When they noticed the way that Chinese soldiers dried their clothing by draping it over cannons, they concluded that the Chinese navy could not fight. We Chinese bluntly refuse to adopt modern attitudes. So whenever we don't feel like doing something, even something as practical as removing our wet clothing from a cannon, we mutter, 'That's not very Chinese'.

The terrible traffic congestion in Taipei is a problem that should and could have been solved a long time ago. If penalties for driving offences were stiff enough, the chaos on the island's public roads would be reduced immediately. But there are a number of people who advocate teaching traffic offenders the rudiments of 'road etiquette', as this is 'more Chinese'. This sort of etiquette has been taken too far. We painted zebra-stripe crossings on the street to aid pedestrians. But then people started getting run over when they walked on them. A friend of mine in Taipei was a totally irresponsible driver. Then he moved to the United States, and because he didn't change his ways, he accumulated so many traffic tickets he almost went broke. Is obeying traffic laws so difficult?

Chinese people are emotionally charged, overly subjective and too often swayed by their moods. They make judgements based solely on their own impressions and experiences. We need to become more broad-minded. We have to learn to look at things from more than one point of view. In physics, the shortest distance between two points is a straight line; in life, that line is inevitably full of twists and turns. We should learn to appreciate life like a connoisseur appreciates a work of art. People can only make distinctions between what is good and bad if they live in a society which values taste and judgement. I remember seeing the opera singer Jiang Miaoxiang perform. She was over 60 at the time, and she had so many wrinkles that she had lost all of her former beauty. But this had no effect on her singing. When she sang 'The Little Cowherd', you forgot her age and her wrinkles disappeared. When Chinese people learn to judge things for themselves, there will be less opportunity for wickedness and evil to thrive in society. If people in our society are ignorant enough to say, 'Bo Yang's paintings are just as good as Van Gogh's', then real artists will have a hard time surviving, and no one in our society will ever produce any great art.

China is a huge country, but Chinese people are petty and narrow-minded. Two days ago, I boarded an airplane at Kennedy Airport in New York. I fell asleep the moment I sat down, but when I woke up an hour later the plane still hadn't taken off. It turned out that the airline had gone on strike. I was amazed at the orderly behaviour of the passengers, who were smiling and talking as if nothing had gone wrong. If an airline went on strike in China, there would be endless shouting and complaints: 'Why haven't we taken off yet? What's going on here? Don't the workers get enough to eat? What's this strike all about? If there's a strike, why did they sell us tickets?' Americans approach things from another angle. They would say, 'If I were an air traffic controller, I'd probably go on strike too'. This gives you an idea about what makes a country great. The United States is a nation built on tolerance. It provides a home for people of every nationality and every colour, people who speak different languages and practise different customs. There's even a place in America for Ugly Chinamen.

I personally have no interest in politics. Nor do I encourage people to get involved in politics. But if you are interested, by all means, get involved, because politics is so important. No matter what you do for a living, one new law can result in the instant disappearance of your money, your freedom, even your life.

Politics is not for everyone. For some people, developing the ability to judge things critically is equally important. Whether we are dealing with politics, literature, or art—especially painting—critical judgement is indispensable. Third-rate painters like Bo Yang are advised to stay put in their studios and keep their paintings to themselves. Otherwise someone who knows something about painting might say, 'You call this art? You have a lot of nerve showing people such crap!' We need to develop the ability to discriminate, otherwise we'll end up living half-arsed lives, and never learn to distinguish good from bad, something that will only serve as an obstacle to progress and growth in Chinese society.

Life, literature and history

Speech given at the History Department, Stanford University, USA, 22 August 1981

I am afraid that the topic assigned to me for this talk, 'Life, literature and history' is a bit over my head. What I plan to discuss are my thoughts about the lessons that 5000 years of Chinese history have taught us.

During my trip to the United States, I have so far visited several Indian reservations and met several American Indians. These visits left me with the impression that the American Indians are possibly facing the threat of extinction.

It sounds absurd to propose the notion that the Chinese people may become extinct some day, firstly since they have such a long history, and secondly because there are so darned many of them. But can anyone give us an ironclad guarantee that the Chinese people will not become extinct?

This is a rather distressing thought, which makes me think about the serious problems facing the Chinese people today. The first question that comes to mind is: why *isn't* China a great country? China has all the preconditions for greatness. I should mention here that I never studied Chinese history formally—actually I learned it the same way Chinese people made steel in their backyard furnaces during the Great Leap Forward: with primitive equipment and lots of sweat.

I'll begin with a story. An American company sent one of its employees to Europe to do some research. When he came back a few months later, he described everything he had seen in a report a couple of hundred pages long. The gist of it was that European technology and management techniques were terribly backward. When the directors of the company read the report, they fired the man immediately. The chairman of the board called him into his office and told him that the reason they had sent him Europe was to learn about those things that European businesses did well, not to pick out their weak points. 'We don't need you to tell us what we are doing right', he said, 'all we want to know is what they do better, so we can improve our products. Praising our products will only put us to sleep. The more we listen to hymns of praise, the sooner the quality of our products will decline, and before long we'll be out of business.'

I haven't come here today to sing the praises of the Chinese people, but rather to talk about the obstacles that stand in the way of China becoming a great nation. Everybody knows how Chinese parents go to extremes to ensure that their children receive a decent education. This has been pointed out so many times that I don't have to say any more about it. Today I am only going to talk about Chinese people's weaknesses. Only by confronting our weaknesses can we begin to improve ourselves.

I

China has a history of 5000 years. But as the centuries rolled by, the respect accorded human dignity only decreased, not increased, under the influence of the Chinese feudal system.

In the Spring and Autumn and Warring States periods (770–221 BC), a ruler and his subjects were considered equals; a king and his ministers could sit together on the same mat. Not until the Western Han dynasty (206 BC–AD 23) did the status of the emperor rise suddenly, in part due to the influence of Confucianism in the court. When ministers attended audience with the Han emperor, armed guards stood beside him, and the slightest infraction of the rules of decorum, such as raising one's head to peek at the emperor's face, was severely punished. As a result the ruler became alienated from the people. At that time, however, ministers could at least sit in the company of the emperor, although on a mat placed below that of the emperor. By the time of the Song dynasty (960–1279), ministers literally had their chairs pulled out from underneath them, and the good old days when the emperor could sit around chatting with his prime minister were no more. In the Ming dynasty (1368–1644), respect for the individual hit new lows with the institution of 'ruler-as-paterfamilias' ideology, according to which the emperor treated all of his subjects as his own children. The endless abuses committed in the name of this practice can easily be imagined.

The worst manifestation of the ruler-as-paterfamilias syndrome was a form of punishment known as cudgelling. Any official, from a prime minister down to the pettiest petty bureaucrat—in fact anyone who wielded a sesame seed's weight of power—who thought you had done something wrong, could bring you to a public place (that could be anywhere from the palace to the town hall), remove your clothing, tie up your arms and legs, and beat you until you were dripping with blood. This form of punishment nearly destroyed Chinese people's self-esteem and had a devastating effect on the Chinese psyche. The only way Chinese people could maintain their dignity while being beaten was to try to refrain from crying out in pain. There are stories about particularly strong-willed officials who rubbed their heads on the ground so vigorously while being beaten in order to suppress their screams, that they scraped all the hair out of their beards. In those days, this was the only way they could respond to this insulting phenomenon. Unfortunately they were unable to co-ordinate their efforts and make a formal protest.

It is common knowledge that the Chinese people have always had strong powers of assimilation, and this remains true today. Throughout history, every nation that has invaded or occupied China has been swallowed up by China in turn. In the Northern Wei dynasty (368–534), the Xiaowen emperor, a member of the Toba clan, adopted the Chinese political system in order to carry out political reform, as did the Manchus 1300 years later. In both cases, powerful barbarian invaders were conquered, in the cultural sense, by China. But while these barbarians ended up adopting Chinese culture (rather than vice versa) we should remember that they assimilated all the worst aspects of Chinese civilisation, with disastrous results. Instead of becoming great, the Tobas and the Manchus degenerated quickly and brought the Chinese down with them.

Audience   What actually is a cudgel?

BY   Basically it means getting spanked on your buttocks. It took four eunuchs to do it properly. First they had you lie on the ground face down. Each of the eunuchs grabbed one of your limbs and tied you up so you couldn't move. Then they put a gunnysack over your head, and two of the eunuchs pressed your legs down on the ground. If the emperor ordered '100 strokes' they beat you 100 times. One hundred strokes was usually the maximum punishment, and certainly enough to kill a man. The dastardly eunuchs in charge of administering the cudgel were highly skilled in feeling out the emperor's intentions. If the Son of Heaven merely detested you, and didn't want you to die, he could order the administration of as many as 200 strokes, and yet allow you to live. But if the emperor had it in for you, the eunuchs could finish you off nicely in 30 or 40 strokes. Most minor officials and petty bureaucrats bribed the eunuchs to ensure that they would be punished with a light hand. There would be plenty of screaming and blood and pain, but the poor victim would survive. Some of these eunuchs were true virtuosi with the cudgel. They could take a paper bag full of straw and strike it in such a way that the straw inside would fragment into bits without the bag breaking. Similarly they could break a man's bones without leaving any marks on his skin. This form of punishment was still being practised in China in the fourteenth and fifteenth centuries, when the Renaissance was taking place in Europe.

We were talking about cultural assimilation. The Mongols were a strange bunch. After they took over China, they adopted a defiant stance in relationship to Chinese culture, and remained locked in this attitude during their 180 years of rule, so that in the end they resisted the influence of Chinese culture. The Manchus inherited all the odious aspects of Chinese culture, politics and social organisation from the Ming, which had a corrupting influence on the newly established state. In fact this influence was so pernicious that the Qing dynasty was doomed only 100 years after its founding. The political and social system engendered by Chinese-style feudalism was so contrary to every notion of human rights that one could say that there was no such thing as human rights in China. Under this system, it was impossible for Chinese people to retain their self-esteem—unless what you call self-esteem is the sort of self-indulgent self-pity exemplified by the protagonist Ah Q in Lu Xun's famous story. The Ah Q mentality and true self-esteem are entirely different kettles of fish.

For example, if you have a beautiful home and are an accomplished scholar, I may respect you and even be jealous of you, which can actually inspire me to emulate you and thus acquire as much knowledge as you have, and eventually live in a nice house like yours. On the other hand, the moment I walk out of your door, I can also say: 'He lives in such a fine house, I wonder where he stole the money to pay for it. The sooner it burns down the better'. This dark side of the Chinese mentality is the result of centuries of oppression. It is the only way many people have to console and comfort themselves when they meet people who are better off than they are.

II

In the last 5000 years, China has had only three golden ages: the first was during the Spring and Autumn and Warring States periods (770 BC–221 BC), when there was a great diversity of thought and lifestyle; the second was a 100-year period during the Tang dynasty, from the reign of Li Shimin to that of Li Lungji (650–756); the third was the first 100 years of the Qing dynasty, from around 1660 to 1760. During the rest of the time—I am talking about more than 4000 years—there was hardly a year, not to mention a day, when China was not at war. A Western scholar once published a set of statistics which showed that never in the history of the world was there a single year when somewhere people were not fighting a war. I did my own research and discovered that this is also true for China. But to compare China with the entire world is unfair. The world is a very big place. Even as late as the Ming dynasty (1368–1644), China controlled as much territory as it had in the second century BC, or about one half as much land as it controls today.

If you consider that during China's extensive recorded history, wars were fought somewhere in China every year—and we're not even talking about minor skirmishes that went unrecorded—the total number of conflicts that took place in the course of Chinese history becomes terrifying to contemplate. The transitional period between dynasties, always a time of chaos, lasted in most cases from thirty to fifty years. A further twenty years was required for the dynasty to consolidate its power. Then came the vicious cycle of corruption, anti-dynastic rebellion, and struggles for dynastic succession. We can even say that from the beginning of their history, the Chinese people have constantly lived in a world of corruption, instability, war, massacres and poverty, something that has left them with a permanent sense of insecurity and anxiety. China's long history and vast territory would tend to make Chinese people broad-minded, worldly and self-confident, but centuries of poverty, human slaughter and jealousy have only left us capable of pettiness and narrow-mindedness. Muddling through is good enough; who knows what will happen tomorrow? There may be a war going on, but who knows when it will end? War means the destruction of the irrigation and canal system, which leads to droughts and locust plagues which leaves the land barren and drives the people to cannibalism. Who can count the number of times the Chinese people have been forced to eat each other? How can civilised people like the Chinese descend to such barbarism? China has suffered countless natural disasters and immeasurable human suffering. We don't have to talk about the Chinese people as a whole; if a single individual is poor for too long or suffers too much, he can easily lose faith in everything.

A few days before I was released from prison in Taiwan, a prison official told me, 'Good news for you, Bo Yang, you're getting out'.

I said to him, 'That's rubbish!'

He said, 'You don't believe me? Why would I lie to you?'

I asked him to show me written proof, because I had believed their lies for so long, and had been deceived so often, that I had given up all hope. Anyone who has suffered long and hard has the right to doubt any good news he hears. The same goes for the citizens of a country. After long periods of suffering, they believe all the promises of good things to come that accompany the advent of a new regime. But before long their hopes will be smashed.

III

One of the oddest aspects of Chinese society, historically speaking, is the Chinese bureaucracy, which evolved from the examination system. Most of you will agree that Japan absorbed Chinese culture in its entirety, from small things like *tatami* (straw mats) and *geta* (wooden clogs) to complex institutions like the imperial system, but there is one important thing that the Japanese did not assimilate from us, that enabled Japan to develop quickly into a major power during the Meiji Restoration, and that is the examination system. The Chinese imperial examination system has its strong points, but it also spawned the Chinese bureaucracy. This bureaucracy is something like spider web, nearly invisible and impalpable, but you always know when you get caught in it. 'Bureaucracy' is not the proper English equivalent for the Chinese institution we are discussing, because the Chinese bureaucracy has its own unique characteristics. The Chinese bureaucrat is loyal neither to his country, nor to the emperor, but only to the bureaucrat who hired him for his job. Chinese dynasties might rise and fall, but the Chinese bureaucracy never changes.

The Manchus succeeded in ruling Tibetans, Mongols and Han Chinese during the Qing dynasty because they knew their adversaries' weaknesses. The Manchus controlled the Tibetans by shrewd manipulation of the Lamaist religion. They invited lamas to Peking and treated them like VIPs. As for the Mongols, the Manchus married their own princesses to Mongol princes—and so their offspring became their nephews and nieces—and raised those princes of mixed blood in the Qing palaces. When they grew up, the Manchus figured these princes wouldn't dare to act naughtily in the presence of their uncles and great-uncles. The Manchu princes themselves scrupulously avoided intermarrying with the Han Chinese, but they kept the Han Chinese in line by means of the examination system. They knew the Chinese people had a fatal flaw: they loved becoming officials more than anything else in the whole world. If a Manchu offered a Han Chinese a chance to be even the pettiest of petty officials, the Chinaman would obey the Manchu for the rest of his life, and give up his national identity and self-respect in the bargain.

The Chinese bureaucracy is very much like a secret society, with its own standards of behaviour and its own values. For Chinese officials, the world was like a school playground where they can bully the younger kids around. Out of this there developed a system of mutual protection that subtly influenced social relations on every rung of Chinese society. From the Chinese point of view, social relations in the United States are embarrassingly simple and straightforward. There's a Chinese saying, 'Getting things done is easy, getting along with others is hard'.

A certain Peking opera has three main characters: a judge, an assessor, and a beautiful young widow whose husband had been murdered. During the murder trial, the widow appears in the courtroom carrying a human head and starts to cry. It is up to the court to identify the head. If it actually belongs to her late husband, the case will be closed quickly. But if it is someone else's head, many people will be implicated in the crime and several executions will take place. The assessor takes a liking to the young widow, and because she hints that she is willing to marry him, the assessor concludes that the head is authentic. Having achieved her goal, the widow rejects the assessor's and advances, so he turns around and declares that the head is a fake. This is a perfect metaphor for Chinese interpersonal relations. The truth gets bandied about like the widow's husband's head; nobody knows what is real or what is fake.

I imagine that many of you have worked in China, or will work there at some point. I can assure you now that the problems you will face there will have little to do with your work itself, but rather with the people you work with. For example, suppose you're working on an atomic reactor. If you don't know the first thing about physics, that's one thing. But let's say you need a specific screw to complete the installation of one phase of the reactor, and the person in charge of the screw department decides to take the day off. He caught a cold, so of course he doesn't have to come to work. You can't force people not to catch colds, can you? Actually, he doesn't have a cold. He's off playing mahjong. Why is he playing mahjong today? Because you and he don't get along, and he doesn't give a damn if your atomic reactor never gets built. 'Let it blow up', he says, 'who cares?' In fact, he'd be very happy to see it blow up in your face. Of course you can say that the national economy will be set back many years. 'What's the hurry?' he says. 'I'm in charge of the screw department.'

Such attitudes have persisted in China for thousands of years, and were still flourishing during the National Revolutionary Army's Northern Expedition in 1928. As the anti-warlord army fought its way north, the evil influence of bureaucracy flowed south. At first the revolutionaries got along extremely well with each other, but their comradely feelings were soon poisoned by the insidious influence of the bureaucracy. In fact all personal relations in those days were as sticky as Superglue. Once you got into a relationship you couldn't get out. How many of you have had this sort of experience? You go back to China and an old friend invites you to a meal. For whatever reason, you do not accept the invitation, and your 'friend' removes your name from his guest-list forever. This is a perfect example of how perverse bureaucratic-style personal relations can be. Why do people behave like this? Why does your 'friend' have to act like a bureaucrat? Because this sort of behaviour reinforces his official status.

A friend of mine went back to Taiwan from the USA for a visit, and was invited to dinner by some people he had never met before. After the meal, the host asked my friend to take some things back to the States for them. The host had not invited my friend to dinner simply to ask him for a favour—a meal in exchange for a delivery—but had made the request as if it were the most natural thing in the world. Sharing a single meal can establish a friendship, and friends are supposed to help each other . . . The Chinese bureaucracy is a weird beast. Let's say you're working on an atomic reactor, a terrifying piece of equipment that only people with specialised knowledge should handle. But the one who invites you to a meal thinks, I'm your friend, so there's no harm in me touching your reactor. People change so radically when they become officials that they become unrecognisable. I know this sounds like nonsense, but the more bureaucratic a person becomes, the less human he is. If you want to deal with a bureaucrat as a human being, you had better wait until he retires from his post.

IV

Confucius was undoubtedly a great man, both cultivated and kind-hearted, who made a significant contribution to mankind. Confucianism, the school of thought that he founded, has had a profound effect on Chinese society over the centuries, and continues to do so today. Confucianism is essentially conservative or, to put it more directly, anti-progressive. The Chinese term 'Confucianism' comes from the word ru, an official in charge of ritual sacrifices. These ru were consulted before every major sacrifice, and as the official guardians of an ancient tradition, were conservative by nature. These ru lived in the days before the new ritual music had come into fashion. Thus in order to keep their jobs, they had to play the same old ritual tunes over and over again. We cannot really call them reactionary 'worshippers of the archaic', which has a negative connotation in Chinese. Let us just say that they were essentially conservative.

Confucianism inhibited creativity, and thus Chinese people did not develop such habits as self-criticism, introspection and self-improvement. Plenty of people bash the United States for killing off the Indians, torturing Blacks, and discriminating against Chinese. These accusations are all based on fact, but what is more important is that Americans are keenly aware of these problems and have taken concrete measures to remedy them. Americans know how to correct their mistakes, an ability Chinese people lack.

The legalist philosopher Shang Yang put his political thought into action when he took over as chief counsellor of the state of Qin. Before his time, entire families slept in the same large bed. Shang Yang wanted the citizens of Qin to be more civilised, so he made a rule that family members had to sleep separately; not even brothers and sisters could share the same bed. This should give you an idea of how barbaric life was in those days. Shang Yang didn't invent the atomic bomb, nor did he do much to improve the people's lives materially. His far-reaching reforms were principally political, social and educational. Shang Yang lived in the fourth century BC. In the ensuing 2000 years, no single Chinese ruler has carried out such radical reforms as Shang Yang, and in fact every ruler that tried has failed. Shang Yang was executed by the genteel method of being tied to two chariots and dismembered. Confucianists have frequently cited the downfall of such reformers as a way of discouraging Chinese people from improving their lot.

The Confucianists had a saying: 'Unless the benefits can be one hundred per cent, there is no need for reform'. Historically this brief statement has been the greatest impediment to progress and greatness in China. No form of change can produce 100 per cent results. At best you can only hope for 50 per cent.

V

The final issue is population. Throughout the course of Chinese history, the founding of a new dynasty was always preceded by a civil war, and followed by a population explosion. And then the whole tragic cycle began again: war, slaughter and death . . .

People say that the living standard in the USA is very high. But the US has a population of only 260 million people. Can you imagine what life would be like in the USA if a billion Chinese people moved there? The population problem is a critical one. If China wants to become a great nation, it must reduce its population dramatically. An old saying goes: 'With a lot of people, it's easy to get things done. With very few people, you can only eat buns'. Chinese buns are steamed, not baked as in the West, and are the cheapest, most basic food there is. In the past, it may have been true that the more people, the easier it was to get things done. But in the modern world, a big population is a burden. A hundred people working together can't accomplish as much as a single computer. The line, 'With very few people, you can only eat buns', also contains a grain of truth. Most people in Taiwan today can afford to raise three children. But what would happen if you acted carelessly and soon found yourself with 200 kids? How would you feed them all?

There are simply too many people in China, poverty is deeply ingrained, the bureaucracy is stultified, and competition is fierce. These factors make Chinese people filthy, sloppy, noisy and contentious. Chinese people don't talk like human beings, they roar like lions! They have lost the ability to act civilly to others.

When I was in Los Angeles, someone asked me my impression of the USA. I told him that I thought America was the politest country in the world. Then he asked me if I thought China was a polite country. I said that China was the most impolite country in the world. Chinese people are crude and backward. They treat others with the gentility appropriate to a blitzkrieg. You may have noticed that Chinese people rarely smile. Is this because they have endured too many disasters, too much suffering, and too many long depressions? By comparison with Chinese, Americans seem like a generally happy bunch. At least those I have met seem to be good-natured, kind and willing to help strangers. By comparison, Chinese people are neurotic, belligerent and paranoid about people taking advantage of them. This makes Chinese people overly cautious, defensive and wary of others, like rats caught in a trap.

People say that there is a lot of racial prejudice in the USA. Of course there's racial prejudice there—what country doesn't have racial prejudice? But notice how the United States tolerates Chinese people. Not only do they tolerate us, they even allow us be rude, dirty, sloppy and noisy and don't get in our way when we engage in clan warfare.

This ends my research report about the United States. We don't have to talk about China's strengths. Whatever we say about them, they won't go away. And if we *don't* talk about them, they won't go away either. I like talking about our faults and weaknesses because it may help us to think a little about ourselves and our problems. China's problems are extremely serious. Our soy paste vat culture is so full of complex problems, it's hard to know what to do about them. What follows are a few of my suggestions.

The first thing we should do in dealing with these problems—if they are indeed problems—is to learn to think for ourselves. For the last several thousand years, other people, such as saints, sages and high-ranking bureaucrats, have done most of our thinking for us. The Chinese never had to use their noggins, nor did they ever dare to use their noggins. How *should* we behave? The more like fools, the better. When Rockefeller's son went exploring in New Guinea and was eaten by cannibals, the newspapers in Taipei published the story. People said, 'Here is someone who had everything going for him, but he threw it all away for nothing. If I were him, I would never have gone to New Guinea.'

When I was in Phoenix, I stayed with an American family for nearly a week. My hosts' sixteen-year-old daughter Margaret had gone to Honduras to teach people there how to protect their eyesight, as the standards of hygiene in Honduras are even lower than those in China—it's a really filthy place. When I was staying in their home, Margaret had just come back from Honduras and was telling her mother about her experiences. She was very excited and announced proudly that she wanted to go back to Honduras the following year, to help the poor and backward people there. Her mother was very encouraging and agreed that she should go.

In a situation like this, most Chinese people would think, 'If I were her, I would never go to a place like Honduras'. But Margaret's mother was proud of her daughter's concern for the welfare of people less fortunate than herself, and her willingness to make sacrifices to help them; her praise was totally sincere.

Compared to people like Margaret, Chinese people are very clever. No ethnic group in the world, not even the Jews, are as shrewd as the Chinese. So shrewd are they, in fact, that once they've been sold off for the kill, they continue haggling over the price of their own flesh all the way to the slaughterhouse. If they can earn five extra bucks before the knife passes through their necks, they will die in ecstasy, knowing they had not lived in vain.

When taken to extremes, cleverness of this sort deteriorates into selfishness. In China, anyone who does something or even thinks something that is not entirely selfish is considered a simpleton. In China, a person who displays the slightest hint of broadmindedness, generosity or consideration, or who has something nice to say about other people, will be cursed as a fool. If someone slaps you in the face, and you protest; or if someone breaks the law and you try to tell him that what he has done is wrong, people will call you an idiot. If you do something that involves taking a risk that prevents you from becoming an official or making a pile of money, everyone will call you a dope. But if we want to save China, we all have to be a little more 'foolish'. Otherwise I fear that Chinese civilisation will disappear like the American Indians. There's an old saying, 'If you are not selfish, heaven and earth will punish you'. Thus anyone who is not selfish will be regarded as a hopeless failure. Each of us should stand on our own two feet, and without the help of the government or other people, do a few things that most people would regard as foolish.

Finally, we ought to try to keep interpersonal relations simple. We can start with our own relationships, and our dealings with our children. For example, when Americans go out for a meal in a fast-food joint, mothers tell their children to clean up their places after they eat and to throw things away in the garbage can. This sort of training can serve as a starting point as well as a goal. Chinese people have numerous virtues, although it's a pity we can only read about them in books. We should try to incorporate them into our lives.

Audience Some things that you have said make me doubtful about the optimism of our generation when we were young. I belong to the generation that grew up after the war. I strongly believe that our generation is different from our parents' generation, in terms of life style, social relations and the way we think. I don't work for the government now, and I can't guarantee that if I become an official someday, I won't turn into one of those cold-blooded bureaucrats you have described. But if I happen to find myself in that situation some day, I hope that I will be somewhat less bureaucratic, and a little more humane, than officials in the past. I doubt that you will agree, though.

Bo Yang I was talking from a historical perspective. Things change with the times, and with improvements in education. Perhaps things are better now. I also respect your sincerity. Actually you would probably make a good official.

Audience I still think your explanation is different from mine.

BY One point I would like to emphasise is that Chinese and Western despotism are very different kettles of fish. I've studied very little Western history, but I am sure there are differences in terms of content as well as degree. Chinese despotism is absolute. In the West, people only kneel down on both knees in God's presence; before the king one knee suffices. In China, you not only had to go down on both knees before the emperor, you had to kowtow too, that is, bang your head on the ground so hard that it was audible. There was a popular saying at the end of the Qing dynasty: 'Kowtow more, talk less'. In a famous portrait of Louis XIV, the king is seated on his throne surrounded by his ministers and queen, who are also seated. This sort of official portrait could never be painted in China. In China any minister who got that close to the emperor would be shaking in his boots and be forced to kneel humbly before the emperor's feet.

Audience   Would you give us your opinion of the simplification of the Chinese written language?

BY   I am very much in favour of simplifying the written language, and I believe Chinese characters should be replaced by a phonetic alphabet. There was a big discussion about this last night, and a lot of disagreement. I think that the people who oppose the idea of simplifying the written language have some sort of mental block. We need a phonetic language urgently. For instance, you make a phone call and ask the person on the other end, 'What's your name?' and he tells you, 'My name is Liu', and you want to know which Liu it is [there are several surnames pronounced 'Liu' in Chinese, each written with a different character], but it's very difficult to explain this over the telephone. If you tell Mr Liu to look up his name in the dictionary, and he fails to find it after three tries, you're sure to lose your temper, since you paid for the call.

In the past we used to complain that classical Chinese texts were unpunctuated, which made it impossible to tell when one sentence ended and the other began. Have you read the *Official History of the Yuan Dynasty*? The long Mongol names in that book look like a bunch of shish-kebabs. It's impossible to tell where one name ends and the next name begins, and how many people they are actually talking about. Modern editions of the classics are punctuated, but this only exacerbates the two major weaknesses in the Chinese writing system. Firstly, words [which are often made up of more than one character] are not separated from each other, so while you may understand all the individual characters in a sentence, you may not be able to figure out all the words. Secondly, because each character is pronounced separately, elision is impossible, and it takes an extraordinary amount of concentration, more than most Chinese people are even aware of, to make sense out of all those rosary beads of sound.

For example, 'I come from Malaysia' in Chinese is written like this: *Wo* (I) *cong* (from) *Ma-lai-xi-ya* (Malaysia) *lai* (come—the same *lai* in *Ma-lai-xi-ya*). In this sentence, the four syllables in 'Malaysia' should be pronounced as one word, and a space left between it and *lai*, come. Otherwise you would have something like *Ma-lai* (the horse cometh) *Xi-ya-lai* (*Xi-ya* comes). If Xi-ya happened to be the name of a child you know, things could get very complicated. Today typewriters and computers operate at such high speeds, I am afraid Chinese characters will never catch up with them. I have often daydreamed about having a Chinese typewriter on my desk, so I could free myself from the task of pushing my pen from one square to the next square on Chinese writing paper.

But romanising the Chinese written language is no mean task. Most people have psychological blocks about it. They think that if you write Chinese with the alphabet it's the same as writing English. But this is a mistaken attitude. Actually A, B, C, D, etc. can be combined to form Chinese words, and Chinese people who do so don't have to feel the shame of being assimilated by the barbarians. No kidding, the Roman alphabet can be Chinese too! Neither English nor German has a monopoly on the alphabet. If you told a German that every time he wrote anything in German he was actually writing English, he would probably blow his top. So would a Frenchman. The letters of the alphabet are simply a tool, like a car. If you buy it, it's yours; if he buys it, it's his. But if we adopted romanised Chinese tomorrow, I'd be one of the first people in China to starve to death, since I still depend on Chinese characters to fill my rice bowl.

Many of you who live in the USA have children who speak Chinese, but can't read or write the language, due to the difficulty of learning Chinese characters. How do you teach them? Take the word *guo* 國 , or 'country' for example. It's actually very complicated when you dissect it, as it is composed of eleven separate strokes or lines. Sometimes I wonder how you squeeze all those lines into one tiny space! The only way to learn Chinese characters is to memorise them by rote, there is no shortcut. When your kids shout, 'I hate Chinese!' doesn't that suggest there's something wrong with the language as it is today?

Should we live our lives for the sake of our ancestors or the past? If we romanise the language, and as a result of this no one can understand the Chinese classics, so be it. How many people can understand the Chinese classics now anyway? As for the past and our ancestors, we can hire a few people to keep the ancestral temples in good order. Our first responsibility is to our children, to the next generation. If Chinese suddenly becomes an international language like English, we would certainly have to romanise it. We could never teach everyone Chinese characters.

Today I've been harping on China's flaws, and by now most of you are probably fed up with me. But I think we should spend more time listening to people talk about our imperfections rather than our virtues. If we go around flattering ourselves, no one will respect us, and it will be hard for us to respect ourselves. Don't forget that the catastrophes that have befallen the Chinese people are not exclusive to China, but affect all mankind. If a small boat capsizes, little damage will be done. But if a huge ocean liner goes down, a lot of other boats will be sucked into the whirlpool and sink. Why did the Japanese invade China? Because the Chinese were too weak to keep them out. It is our own duty to save China, and save ourselves. To do this, we must first understand our faults and weaknesses. If we go around with our noses in the air, it's no better than living in a wet dream.

PART II
Bo Yang writes

Signs and symptoms of Chinese cultural senility

Too cowed to crow

I don't recall which clever ancient Chinese gentleman it was who spawned that magnificent conception, the eunuch. Eunuchs are men, to be sure, but once their penises are chopped off, they take on the qualities one expects from a friend: useful, not threatening. Such a brilliant invention! Chinese emperors were enthralled by their eunuchs, and thus they became one of those venerable Chinese institutions that survived for thousands of years.

Alas! Confucius said, 'Be benevolent', and Mencius said, 'Be righteous'. I hate to bring it up, but it seems to me that chopping off a man's penis is neither benevolent nor righteous. The odd thing is that throughout the centuries, not a single enlightened Chinese sage, including the eminent philosophers Zhu Xi and Wang Yangming, ever suggested that there was anything improper about reducing healthy young men to eunuchs. I also find it quite amazing that numerous Chinese sages, with their predilection for censuring improper behaviour, never raised their sanctimonious voices to chastise the emperor for depriving so many good men of their penises, and simply pretended that the practice didn't exist.

I can think of two explanations for this. First, some of the great sages of the past were well aware of the unseemliness of this practice, but kept their mouths shut because the emperors had invented the institution of eunuchs to protect themselves from cuckoldry. Had one of these enlightened sages succeeded in persuading the emperor to replace his eunuchs with a bunch of handsome, well-endowed young men, the number of incidents of imperial cuckoldry would have increased strikingly, and the emperor would have regularly flown into a rage. The only way out for a sage who committed a sin of this magnitude would be to swallow a large dose of arsenic. Throughout Chinese history, even heroes courageous enough to swallow raw pork would pretend that they had never seen the emperor ordering men to have their penises chopped off.

Secondly, for the last 5000 years, lords, vassals, saints and sages alike have all been much too preoccupied with muddling their way though life to concern themselves with the moral niceties of this cruel variation on decapitation. Chinese culture fails to inspire the sort of insight necessary for making moral judgments of this nature. The emperor had the power to execute anyone he pleased. What did slicing off a few penises amount to when whacking off a thousand heads was the most natural thing in the world? Humanitarian values disappear under reigns of terror, and the slave mentality thrives. The wise man would say, 'As long as you make me a petty official, I'll approve of anything you do, no matter how horrible it is'.

(from *Unenlightened*)

Self preservation uber alles

A wise man once said: 'He who knows something but does not act upon it does not possess true knowledge'. If you recognise the importance of co-operating with others, but don't co-operate with others yourself, then you don't recognise the importance of co-operation. This weakness is not inherent in the Chinese personality, but rather results from regularly overdosing on Confucian medicine and suffering from chronic indigestion. Actually Confucianism advocates individualism rather than the 'mass line'. When Professor Confucius lectured to all those second-class sages who advocated 'universal education', you could call it 'educating the masses', but one actually finds Confucius talking about universal education about as frequently as one finds pearls in oysters. Clearly most of Confucius' teachings encouraged individualism. The Confucians seemed to have two lofty aspirations: one was to teach the common people to keep their heads stuck in the sand, their tails tucked between their legs, and their noses out of politics. The masses were encouraged to spend the bulk of their energy protecting their families and their property, putting into practice those old adages, 'A rational man protects himself first' and 'He who understands all the implications of a given situation is a hero'. This doctrine basically encouraged Chinese people to take the line of least resistance whenever possible.

The second aspiration was to try to encourage those in power to show mercy to the helpless common people, and to beseech officials to go easy when trampling on their heads. The relevant adage was: 'Practise benevolent government.'

Confucius had a brilliant philosophy for avoiding calamities. In plain language: 'Avoid dangerous societies. Don't live in dangerous communities. In times of social stability, take an official position. In times of chaos, distance yourself from society. In prosperous times, if you don't take an official position, you should feel shame. In bad times, if you have an official position, you should also feel shame.'

These sage teachings are excellent guidance for shrewd, slippery characters who follow the crowd. Once others have gone to the trouble of creating social stability, they leap on board and become officials. But when everyone has to risk life and limb to protect the state, they're busy greasing up the soles of their boots, so they can slip away quietly and make a killing during the chaos, as everyone else is too busy trying to survive.

The most exemplary orthodox Confucians are Chinese parents who send their children to the United States to 'propagate'. They would fit in nicely as the directors of the Confucius and Mencius Institute. They know that in the mind of the true snob, bootlickers are the only virtuous people, because only they can make snobs feel at ease with themselves. Confucius said: 'The son of a wealthy man does not sit beneath a tottering roof'. Chinese intellectuals avoid putting themselves in situations where there is even the slightest risk of 'a tile falling off the roof'. If there is official corruption, or if the common people are suffering from some injustice, they will pretend it doesn't exist, because it has nothing to do with them. Confronted by corruption and injustice, they will feel righteous indignation, and be inspired to speak out, but this will only land them in deep trouble. It is a tragedy for China that in all the Confucian teachings, there is little encouragement for intelligent thinking, scarce mention of the responsibility incumbent upon people in authority, and almost no stimulus for competition. Confucius only wanted his disciples, and his disciples' disciples, to accept the status quo, and to remain smug and self-satisfied. You could do as you pleased, as long as you never took risks. Confucius had few good words for anyone except Yan Hui, who hardly had a penny to his name. Confucius praised Yan Hui's stoicism in the face of extreme poverty, but he didn't question society's role in impoverishing this second-class sage; nor did he seek ways to reduce suffering in society, with its teeming masses of poor people. Rather, he taught people to be happy even though they were poor. When everyone in China is *that* happy, Chinese society will have regressed to the age of the troglodytes.

(from *Crashing into the Soy Paste Vat*)

The animal that cannot smile

I used to think that all Oriental people had a congenital disability that prevented them from smiling. However, when I visited Japan I was pleased to discover that the Orientals who inhabit that island nation are not only adept at smiling, but also seem to derive great pleasure from it. Not only do Japanese bus conductresses smile, even the girls who operate those coffin-like elevators are accomplished smilers. Wondering why Chinese people don't smile, I considered such factors as the many wars that have been fought in China over the last 150 years, and how, obeying the laws of natural selection, Chinese people learned to respond by crying rather than laughing. Of course there were other factors to consider as well, such as hunger, chronic shortages of material goods, and so on.

The inability to smile has a deleterious effect on the tourism industry. The most serious consequences of this flaw are related to Chinese people's behaviour towards strangers. I've travelled to nearly every corner of China, and with the sole exception of Beijing, there wasn't a single place where strangers were not given a hard time.

Homo sapiens are the only mammals that smile—the only exception being Chinese nurses and female bus-ticket sellers. The humble citizens of Taiwan have been complaining about this glum situation for more than a decade, but the authorities who run the bus company and the hospitals seem to have been too busy taking bribes to pay any attention to their complaints. It's nearly impossible to squeeze a smile out of these virtuosi of the frown unless you throw money directly in their faces.

Female sales clerks' faces could do with a bit of improvement as well. The moment you walk into the shop, they glare at you with their beady eyes as if you were a cat intruding upon their private rat's lair. When you ask to see something in the shop, they'll appraise your clothing and say something like, 'This is very expensive', or in plain Chinese, 'I don't think you can afford that'. If you ask, 'Do you have anything else of similar quality?', they'll shoot back with, 'Yes, but it's even more expensive'. During his student days, a friend of mine who was at a college of foreign languages had a particularly bad experience shopping in a commission store in Taipei. After he had picked out a NT$500 sweater, the owner of the store glanced at my

friend's school pin and said to him, 'When you graduate from translation school and get a job, at most you'll earn five or six hundred a
month. You ought to save your money.' Imagine how surprised the store
owner was when my friend decided to buy that sweater. Even more
discomfitting is when you examine a few items in a shop and leave
without buying them. Everyone from the owner down to the lowliest
clerk sends you away with a dirty look, and they start mumbling to
themselves as if they'd just been buggered.

I've heard claims that the very same shopkeepers and sales clerks
always smile when a foreigner comes into the store. But it should be
pointed out that as tourism develops in Taiwan and the number of
foreign tourists increases, at least one or two impoverished foreigners
are bound to appear on the local tourist circuit. By that time, the Ugly
Chinaman syndrome will have spread and intensified, and before long
foreigners will be treated the same way as Chinese.

One thing we Chinese can be proud of is the way taxi drivers in
Taiwan don't accept tips, but a single isolated virtue is hardly enough
to stimulate the tourist industry. The admirable 'one price, no bargain-
ing' system practised in many shops should be adopted more widely.
When I find myself in a store with jacked-up prices, where getting a
fair deal depends entirely on luck, I try to extricate myself by offering
a price so low that the seller is forced to refuse. Little did I know . . .
In one shop, I was looking at a suitcase marked $300, but I knew that
at best it was worth only $150. I really didn't like the way it was
designed, so I offered $70. Much to my horror the clerk said, 'OK, it's
yours'. I thought he would have committed suicide sooner than sell it
to me for such a low price.

A land of rites and righteousness

The level of an individual's self-cultivation, and the moral fibre of an
entire nation, reveal themselves in even the most superficial social
situations. In the novel *Records of Flowers in the Mirror*, Tang Ao
judges whether a country is civilised or not according to whether old
people and young children are cheated in shops. When he found a place
where they were not cheated, he was so impressed that he went down
on his knees and kowtowed.

In the United States, people take it for granted that they won't be
cheated when they shop. In American shops, prices are fixed fairly to
begin with, while the service tends to be remarkably good.

When we were in Las Vegas my wife went into a small shop and
bought herself a jacket for twelve dollars. She paid for it, but while

the saleswoman was wrapping it up, my wife discovered a black spot about the size of a grain of rice on the right sleeve near the armpit. She said, 'Aiyah, what's this?'

The saleswoman, a pleasant old lady, looked at the black spot and said apologetically, 'There's a spot on it, all right. You can probably wash it out with soap and water, but it may be permanent. If you don't mind, I'll go ask the boss and see if we can't take a few dollars off the price for you.' She went upstairs, and when she came down, she told my wife they would sell it to her for ten dollars.

This was the most absurd thing I ever heard. In fact, I'm so accustomed to being taken for a ride by sadistic merchants that I take it for granted when I'm overcharged. When my wife told me about this little incident, I had an urge to grab that saleswoman and kiss her smack on the lips.

Had this taken place in Taipei, or Hong Kong, it would have been a lot more like a cops and robbers story. If a bitchy customer started picking faults with the 'superior merchandise', the salesperson would come up to her with her bloodshot eyes and cackle, 'Eh? What's that? A black spot? Are you pulling my leg? You don't think I can see it with my own eyes, do you? Even if there is a black spot there, it's hidden under the armpit, what's the difference? Are you one of those people who goes around showing off your armpits all the time? If you want be picky, you should have told me you didn't want the jacket before I wrote out the sales slip. Not everyone's as sneaky as you. You want to return it now? You want a discount? You're an odd sort, aren't you, the next time you go shopping, you ought to count how much money you have in your pocket first, and not go around pretending you're some sort of rich bitch. Oh, you're still not satisfied? We Chinese have a 5000-year-old tradition of practising the rites and dispensing righteousness; we always try to make our customers feel at home. You mean to tell me you don't feel at home here? You look pathetic. What's the matter now, you think somebody's trying to cheat you? You think our company can't survive without your ten cent purchase? You hicks from overseas don't have no culture. It's not even worth the trouble calling the cops. All right, you know as well as I do that you can't afford that, so give it back to me!'

Las Vegas is a gambling town. Ninety-nine per cent of the people who go there are tourists, and 99 per cent of those tourists will only visit Las Vegas once or twice in their lifetimes. So if a shopkeeper wants to cheat a customer, he has little reason to lose sleep over it. But my wife was treated with the same cordiality and honesty there as in stores elsewhere in the United States.

(from *Stepping on His Tail*)

Three polite phrases

The most severe cultural shock most Chinese experience when they go to the United States is the variety and complexity of American etiquette. If you ever-so-gently rub shoulders with someone on the street—so gently that you can't be sure you actually touched each other—the average American will turn around and say, 'I'm sorry'. If you do bump into each other, and really feel it, then the straightforward 'I'm sorry' gets transformed into a profound lamentation. And if you actually smack into each other with a bang, you'll be offered a whole string of sincere 'sorry's. This semi-automatic 'sorry' response is the sort of kindness that kills.

When two Chinese collide on the sidewalk, it's an entirely different sort of affair. The reaction comes lightning-fast and the repartee rumbles like thunder. Mr A will start jumping up and down as if he were competing in a high jump. Inevitably his first words will be, 'Are you blind, or what?' to which the answer will be, 'Hey, it was an accident. Who bumped into who anyway? When you bumped into me, I didn't say a thing, so why get so hot under the collar?'

Mr A will then raise his voice one octave higher and say, '*You* ran into me, so what makes you so nasty? Didn't your parents teach you how to behave in public?' Mr B will then turn up the volume further: 'Bumping into you isn't committing murder, is it? You want me to get down on my knees and kowtow to you? You say *I* bumped into you? That's preposterous, I never bump into people. *You* bumped into me. You're trying to put the blame on me?' At this juncture, the more civilised types will go their own way muttering obscenities to themselves, while the less civilised will escalate the conflict to a fist fight, and attract a large audience of eager boxing fans.

The reader will notice that from start to finish neither party uttered a single 'Sorry' or 'Excuse me'. That cardinal Ugly Chinaman virtue, never admitting errors, finds perfect expression in this sidewalk vignette. The Chinese people have lost the ability to say 'I'm sorry', and like rocket engines have to depend on force to attain their goals.

One admirable characteristic of Western civilisation is the way people acknowledge each other's existence, and treat each other with respect. This makes them conscientious about being polite to others all the time. If someone steps on your foot, it's 'Sorry'. If someone doesn't step on your foot but almost steps on your foot, it's still 'Sorry.' If someone coughs, he will say 'Excuse me', and if he sneezes, it's 'Excuse me' too. If he has to take a piss in the middle of a conversation, naturally it's 'Excuse me'. And if a fire breaks out in his kitchen when you are having dinner at his house, and he rushes away from the dining table in order to put it out, it's 'Excuse me' once again.

Foreign visitors in the United States often have the following experience: some Americans are taking pictures of each other, and while they're posing you happen to get between the camera and the person being photographed without being aware of it. But even then you get a polite 'Sorry.' And if you're taking a picture, most Yankees will freeze in their tracks with a big smile on their faces and wait until you're finished before proceeding. If it's Chinese people who are taking pictures, you'll never get any reaction out of them if you go out of your way to avoid getting in the picture. In such situations, Chinese people are very much like wooden Indians. But if a gregarious American's taking a picture, and you stop in your tracks in order not to be in the way, you'll get a full-blown 'Thanks a lot'.

Actually I find 'Thanks a lot' just as life-threatening as 'I'm sorry'. It's hard to believe that people can waste so much breath and energy on these two phrases. As everyone knows, I'm a martial arts expert, but when I first visited the USA, none of the eighteen routines I have mastered enabled me to escape from their persistent 'thanking' and 'sorrying'. In fact, the more I tried to escape, the more people said 'Thank you'. When Americans buy something in a shop, it's the customer who says 'Thank you'. (In China, a customer would never say 'Thank you'. If a salesperson ever thanked a customer, the roof would be so moved it would collapse.) In the US, when you withdraw money from your bank account, the teller will say 'Thank you'. (Try this in any bank in China, and you'll immediately get homesick for the West.) If you break the speed limit or make an illegal left turn, the policeman will thank you when he hands you the ticket.

But the most impressive 'Thank you' I ever experienced was part of the 'strange case of the spring door'. Whenever I go through a door with a spring, I simply let the door go after I walk in or out. But you can't do that with spring doors in the USA, they're different. When I first arrived in the USA a friend warned me, 'Now that you're in barbarian territory, you better throw away all of your 5000-year-old cultural baggage. Whenever you go through a spring door, make sure you turn around and see if anyone is coming in after you, and then let the door close slowly.'

Have you ever heard anything so preposterous? I went to the United States as a tourist, not as a doorman. I'd opened more spring doors in my time than my friend had ever set eyes on. What gave him the idea he could teach me how to do it? And then one day I understood what he was talking about. I was passing through a spring door and let it go, as was my habit. Suddenly an old man who had been walking behind me let out a scream. My friend and I were so embarrassed that we wanted to get down on our knees and kowtow to him as a way of showing our apologies. (Actually I had tried to slip away unnoticed, but a crowd gathered so quickly it was impossible to make a clean getaway.) Fortunately the impact of the swinging door hadn't dislodged any of his soft brain matter: the old man stared at me from head to toe, and realising that I was a VIP from a tribe of New Guinea head hunters, decided to drop the whole matter.

After this incident, my friend told me, 'You don't have to know *why* Americans do things the way they do. Just imitate them, like a good Chinaman'. Only then did I attain an awareness that the Western Way of the Door requires one to stand aside, hold the door open, and allow the person behind you to go in before you.

Another technique I had to learn was how to release the door gently so the next person coming in could get a hold of it before it closed, something akin to passing the baton in a relay race. You *can* teach an old dog new tricks and before long I became a door virtuoso. From that day on, every time I opened a door the American way I enjoyed the exquisite pleasure of hearing the tender echo of an old woman's 'Thank you' in my ears.

When I got back to Taipei, I continued to open doors the American way but gave it up after only three days. No, my mind had not deteriorated. Every time I held a door open and stood back to let someone pass, those honourable descendants of the Yellow Emperor gave me a look that suggested they had a three-day-old turd stuck in their throat. Not a single person said 'Thank you' to me. So I went back to my old habit of letting the door swing wildly, unconcerned with whether the idiot it smacked in the face lived or died! I resigned myself to the fact that the only way to pry a simple 'Thank you' out of a Chinese mouth was with a set of dentist's tools.

'Thank you' and 'I'm sorry' are fixtures of daily life in democratic countries, and even children who are just learning to talk say 'Thank you' to their mothers when they change their nappies. At the same time, I feel that Americans go a bit overboard with politeness. You've seen bank robberies on TV, no doubt. A muscular hunk, gun in hand, orders the teller to fill his briefcase with money, and then tips his hat and says 'Thank you' before he leaves. In the end, methinks it is preferable to go overboard in this respect, rather than choke to death on a dried-out turd.

I forgot to mention that 'Thank you' and 'Sorry' are always accompanied by a big smile, and are often followed by that other notable phrase, 'May I help you?' Mind you, a man of my age and experience—born on mainland China, living in Taiwan; wandered from the mountains to the cities, from tiny hamlets to huge universities, progressed from babbling to ranting and raving—though on occasion I have heard people in China say 'Sorry' and 'Thank you', I swear to Confucius that never in my entire lifetime have I heard anyone say 'May I help you?'

When we visited the United States, friends picked us up in their fancy cars almost every time we went out. One evening, however, my wife and I took the Metro from downtown Washington to Springfield, Virginia. Springfield is the last station on the line, and from there we had to take a taxi the rest of the way. You know how difficult it can be to find a taxi in some American cities, and when the sun disappeared behind the western hills, we became as nervous as two stray dogs.

A young American man who had noticed our predicament came over and asked, 'May I help you?' Was he addle-brained or what? We obviously needed help so he put down his briefcase, stood in the middle of the road, and after much gesturing, got a taxi to pull over. The driver, it seemed, was on his way home for dinner, and started to give the young man a hard time. But our friend persisted, and after a few moments waved to us and told us to get in the car. Before I had a chance to ask him his name and thank him, he was gone. If it hadn't been for him, we probably would have had to spend the night in the Metro station.

(from *Stepping on His Tail*)

The land of the queue

Before going to the United States, my wife injured her back. To ease her recovery, she brought along a woven cane seat-back. She had used this seat-back for over six months in Taiwan, but it had never attracted anyone's notice. After we arrived in the United States, it began to perform wonders. Everywhere she went, older Americans treated her with amazing consideration. They seemed to think her back was about to snap in two like a chopstick. On airplanes and trains, the moment she stood up or even leaned forward in her seat, people would come up to her and say, 'May I help you?' She really wanted to say, 'No you can't help me, I have to go to the toilet'. Could someone possibly go to the toilet for her? After this happened a few times, whenever she had to go to the toilet, she repressed the urge in order not to appear ungrateful.

This kind of consideration for others is entirely unknown in Chinese society. What's worse, anyone who goes out of their way to help others is dubbed a 'busybody'. And if someone is having a hard time, and you help them out, people will be sure to launch a sidewinder missile in your direction, and attack you with such well-worn adjectives as 'meddlesome', 'nosey', 'intrusive', etc. . . . Furthermore, anyone who acts in such an unorthodox fashion will be accused of having ulterior motives. I'll bet a dollar that if you're on a street in Taipei throwing up or suffering from an attack of dysentery, no one will lift a finger to help you.

About a year ago I went to the movies in Taipei with an American acquaintance of mine. In the middle of the picture, a man in the audience started foaming at the mouth and collapsed in the aisle. A few minutes later, two men came into the theatre and carried him out. We assumed that they were going to take him to the hospital, but when the movie was over and we left the theatre, we noticed him lying on the ground in an alley in the same condition he had been in when he first had his attack. Lying there he looked more like a primitive tribesman who had been captured by an enemy tribe than a Son of the Celestial Dragon. Hundreds of people walked by him, but no one stopped to help. My American friend observed, 'Chinese people are almost as cold and heartless as New Yorkers'.

It was very clever of him to have qualified his comparison with an 'almost'. If he hadn't, ardent Chinese patriots would have found his remark rather far-fetched, even sarcastic, and might have accused my friend of 'stirring up animosity between the government and the people'. He chose New York City because it is one big campsite inhabited by a greater number of ethnic minorities who won't forget their roots than in any other city in the USA. Actually, about 80 per cent of New Yorkers are ethnic minorities, which is why many Americans like to pretend that New York City isn't part of the USA.

As I was saying, if you are Chinese, and you live in China, it is extremely difficult to help people in distress. And, as I have said elsewhere, people with low ethical standards cannot understand people with high ethical standards, nor can they imagine others having high ethical standards.

One cold and rainy evening, another friend of mine who drives a taxi in Taipei picked up a woman who was drenched from head to toe and shivering so hard her teeth were chattering. He had just picked up a sweater and pair of woollen pants belonging to his wife at the cleaners, and out of consideration for her discomfort, said to her, 'Miss, why don't you take off your wet clothing and change into these? You can give them back to me when you get home and change into something dry.' But the woman only heard the part about taking off her clothes, and screamed at the top of her voice, 'Dirty old man! I'll report you to the police!' My friend was so angry that he shouted back, 'Then I hope you catch TB'.

Another friend of mine, a teacher, was on a bus one day when he noticed that the handle of a woman's (sorry, it's a woman again!) parasol had fallen off and was about to be stepped on by another passenger, so he picked it up and made his way to the back of the bus to give it back to her. Thank Buddha that this woman had a decent streak in her, and declined to call my friend a dirty old man. But she didn't thank him, or say anything to him, just stared at him with one of those looks you see on the face of a fish in the market on a hot summer afternoon. Chinese people seem to have evolved as far as troglodytes, and stopped there. They're always fully armed, like porcupines, projecting hostility and jealousy from their anxious eyes, as if they don't have a friend in the world.

Returning to the topic of my wife's cane seat-back, not only did it elicit numerous offers of help from Americans everywhere, it also guaranteed her a place at the head of every queue she joined. I've always felt that the queue is an ideal barometer for measuring how civilised a country is. Though I only spent two months in the USA, I was about to suggest changing the name of that country from the United States of America to the United Queuers of America. In the USA, not only is queuing a national compulsion, it's a national disaster, and I can only pity all those obedient people who waste precious time lining up in neat rows. In the USA they queue up to get on airplanes, get off airplanes, have their luggage inspected, have their passports inspected, buy stamps, mail letters, buy tickets, withdraw money from the bank, wait for the bus, get on the bus, go to the toilet, and what's worse, they even queue up at restaurants.

I'm not boasting, but I really don't mind queuing up. In fact, no Chinese minds queuing up. However, it should be stated clearly that American and Chinese queuing are quite different in terms of form and content. In China, queuing up is an abstract concept, while in the USA it's a way of life. In Taipei the locals practise a sort of quasi-queuing. They'll line up in an orderly fashion at a bus stop, but the moment the bus appears, all chaos breaks out. The brawny types cut a bloody path through the crowd and claim all the seats, while the old, the infirm, the handicapped and the war veterans, bearing the scars of battle, bring up the rear. Why queue in the first place? Exerting brute force is perhaps understandable when it is a question of getting a seat for a long ride, or a matter of getting on an already overcrowded bus. But I'll never understand why we Chinese still fight to get on a bus or train when all the seats are reserved. The seats certainly aren't going to fly away, and if someone takes your seat, it's not as if their bottom is nailed to it permanently. What's all the fuss about?

Americans seem resigned to queuing up for the rest of their lives, and suffer it with admirable equanimity. In China, with its vast population, queues are so long and tightly packed, with Mr A's nose jabbed into Mr B's neck, that they resemble a bunch of army veterans heading into battle together. By comparison, Americans seem a bit lazy, even passive, when they line up. If a queue in America extends across a thoroughfare or in front of a garage entrance, it will spontaneously and politely break at that point to let a car through. When I see such depressing scenes as this, I become very pessimistic about the future of the United States.

When I was in New York, I went with a friend to withdraw some money at a bank renowned for being crowded. Perhaps my friend had heard about my fabled martial arts exploits on crowded buses in Taipei, and wanted me to show off in front of the Americans. When we got there, I noticed that there was one long queue, and only one person transacting their business at each window. Naively I headed for one of these one-man queues, anticipating that I would complete my business in a matter of minutes. Within three seconds, however, my friend had grabbed me by the scruff of the neck and pulled me away as if he had nabbed a thief. He apologised for such rough handling, and then shouted at me, 'What the hell are you doing?'

I replied, 'What am I doing? I'm queuing up at the bank, what do you think I'm doing? Every day since I arrived in your blessed country, I get blamed for something I do. Don't tell me lining up in a bank is against the law?'

'It's not against the law, but it is against bank regulations.' I then learned that you had to line up in that long queue and wait your turn before hopping up to the 'next available teller' like a bunny rabbit. Poor America! Such a young country, but so many regulations! Certainly so much red tape will sap the American people's morale.

The most exasperating queues are those that form in front of restaurants. Ever since Pan Gu divided the sky from the earth, no one in China has ever queued up to get into a restaurant. The first time I ate in a restaurant in San Francisco, I walked in the front door and was just about to take a seat at a table when I was hauled back into the lobby by my wife. There was no queue there, and no other people waiting. What rule had I broken this time? Then I learned that even if there are no ghosts, not to mention people, waiting to be served, you still have to stand around until the hostess shows you to your seat, which she did that night as coolly as if she were retrieving two corpses from the fridge. Had no one shown us our seats, we would have starved to death waiting. But a worse fate awaited us had we taken our seats by ourselves.

My clearest memory is of a little restaurant near the Grand Canyon in Colorado, where few places stay open for dinner. God had blessed us, as it was unnecessary to queue here, but you did have to go to the counter, put down your name, and then wait near the door to be called. Whenever the hostess appeared before us hungry 'waiters', we all looked up at her, trembling in awe and fear, as if she were the Mother of Jesus come to relieve our distressed souls. As she read out each name, the members of the 'chosen' family broke into jubilant shouting, as if they had been summoned to the Pearly Gates. Much ado about nothing, if you ask me.

In Taipei we do things our own way. Like a bunch of starved prisoners, customers continue to force their way into restaurants even though it's perfectly obvious the place is already packed to the rafters. They scout out a table where the plates are nearly empty—a sign that the people sitting there are about to leave—and surround it. Those seated at the table, seasoned veterans of these guerilla tactics, continue to enjoy their meal without raising an eyelid, while the invading forces gaze enviously at the mouths chomping away leisurely at the delicacies set out before them. Finally, having eaten to their fill, the front-line squadron takes its leave and is replaced at the table by the starving guerillas, who before long are surrounded by another wave of invading forces. This scene reminds me of the way a wolf in the African prairie raises its head and watches as an alligator chews its quarry with obvious satisfaction.

It is tragic that Chinese restaurants in the United States have started to adopt the practice of queuing and are gradually doing away with the traditional Chinese form of voyeurism known as 'going to the eaties'.

Everyone says the United States is a free country. I beg to differ. In America you even have to queue up to go crazy.

So this is what you call a civilised country?

On paper, China is a highly civilised country. In the flesh, however, Chinese people are barbarians.

Some day, perhaps, China will become civilised. That is one of my greatest hopes. A wise old friend of mine said to me, 'So you think China is a *fake* civilised country, like a fake Rolex watch?'

'I don't mean that,' I replied. 'China doesn't qualify for fake-civilised status yet. It's too primitive and barbaric.'

He almost fainted when I said that, and I only saved him from smashing his skull by placing a chair under his rapidly descending derrière, and when he landed on it he sat there gasping for breath. Sadly enough, there are another billion gasping Chinese patriots where he came from. Better ignore their gasping, and judge for yourself how barbaric the Chinese are, without allowing your emotions to cloud your judgement.

Scene One: a Chinese wedding

Even movie stars with countless divorces to their credit seem to take marriage seriously. Otherwise, why do they bother going through the same old ceremony again only months after their last divorce? A marriage is a great leap forward, a significant breakthrough in life. Both partners must give up their former existence, board a brand new ship, as it were, reorganise their lives around each other, and sail off into uncharted waters with all four hands on the tiller. Marriage causes so many radical changes in life that it is always regarded as a solemn occasion, be it celebrated in traditional Chinese style or with a Western-style church wedding. We don't have to go back very far; even in the 1940s, Chinese peasant weddings were major undertakings. The groom would go by sedan chair or car to the bride's house—this was called 'welcoming the bride'. The couple would then be carried back to the groom's home, where they offered up three prayers: the first to heaven and earth to thank the gods for arranging their match; the second to the groom's parents to thank them for raising him; and the third to each other, after which they became man and wife.

The same basic procedure takes place in a church wedding. The solemn strains of the 'Wedding March' can fill the air, and the groom takes up his position before the altar. The bride walks slowly down the aisle on her father or brother's arm, and when they reach the altar her father or brother 'gives the bride away'. Then the minister or priest pronounces them man and wife in the name of God.

Several years after the fall of the Qing dynasty in 1911, Chinese people invented a non-traditional, non-religious form of ceremony called the 'civilised civil wedding'. Evidently the marrying types of the day decided that kowtowing was too old-fashioned, and churches too 'foreign', so they replaced weddings with free-for-all farces that closely resembled the goings on in a bazaar or a temple fair. Few guests at civilised weddings concerned themselves with celebrating the solemn and joyous occasion; it was more like going to the circus. Some guests ignored the wedding altogether, and merrily socialised with their friends. Even though these guests lived in the same city, some of them only got together once every few years, and so the wedding hall gradually came to serve the function of a restaurant or teahouse. When the wedding ceremony ended, out came the mahjong tables, and the party began: people made business appointments, talked about their latest escapades, exchanged gossip, recalled the good old days, and swore at their enemies. When the best man got up and tried to make a polite speech, it was so noisy that even though he shouted at the top of his voice, no one in the room could hear what he was saying. The matchmaker, who was often brought in at the last minute, usually forgot the bride's name as well as the sacred nature of his duties. When addressing the wedding guests, he would start telling jokes about everything that took place in the bridal chamber on the wedding night. Chinese matchmakers spiced their humour with so many obscenities that if the editor of *Playboy* magazine had been present, he would have called in the vice squad.

Everyone who attends such weddings gets caught up in the circus atmosphere, so to compare a 'civilised wedding' to a Chinese vegetable and meat market is rather generous. Actually weddings are occasions especially arranged for the bride and groom's families and friends to suffer insults and for God to weep in commiseration.

Scene Two: a Chinese funeral

A death is an even more solemn occasion than a marriage and, unlike marriage, you only get one chance to go through with it. Death is the ultimate, eternal conclusion of life. A man lives a long life and suffers much, but at the end he must part with his beloved ones forever. The funeral parlour is the last stop on his life's journey. The next step is to take up permanent residence in the cemetery. A funeral should be a solemn and dignified occasion. In ancient China, there was a saying, 'The mourners were greatly pleased', which referred to their satisfaction that the funeral rites had been carried out with due attention to propriety. It did not mean that they were celebrating someone's death, or that he had died at a convenient moment.

Funerals these days consist of the following ritual: upon entering the funeral parlour, the guests bow before the coffin and offer their last respects, while the immediate relatives of the deceased kneel on the ground and kowtow before the coffin. If the widow is elderly and the children are very young, there will be much crying and wailing and moaning; it's all very sad and tragic. Once this part of the ritual is over, the guests will walk away from the coffin, head for the first familiar face, and start off with something like, 'Hey Jack, I've been trying to get in touch with you, how long has it been? Been going to too many of these goddamned funerals and weddings lately, haven't had a free afternoon in months. How about going out and getting a bite to eat?'

Just as the two of them are heading out the door, a certain Presence looms up before them, and these two reptiles fall over each other as they attempt to be the first to say, 'Minister X, I do hope all is well with your excellency'. The minister nods and smiles, shakes their hands politely, and then glides into the funeral parlour. The reptiles instantly revise their plans, and tag along after the minister with broad smiles on their faces. The moment the Presence makes his entrance, all the other guests start to crowd around him, and within seconds the funeral parlour turns into a clubroom. But even if the Presence had not appeared, the funeral would soon have turned into a clone of the 'civilised wedding' described above. Few people who attend weddings are sincerely disposed to grieving, and the atmosphere resembles something like a holiday bazaar. The problem is, when so many people who know each other get together, a certain amount of socialising is inevitable. Foreign observers often criticise Chinese people for being cruel and unfeeling. The sad thing is, a funeral is really intended to be an occasion for widows and their children to mourn a painful loss, and for God to suffer distress.

Scene Three: the Chinese restaurant

Nowhere else can you observe such a range of Chinese ritualistic behaviour as in Chinese restaurants. Actually the quintessence of Chinese etiquette is the 'war of two battles' that takes place at every Chinese banquet.

The first of these battles is called 'the battle of the seats'. At every banquet, one guest is chosen to sit at the place of honour. Usually he or she is an important official, or just filthy rich. But the guest of honour likes to pretend that there's a poisonous snake hiding under the cushion of the chair of honour, and will make a show of refusing to sit there. When he does this, all the other guests, including the host, surround him and with pushing and shouting try to get him to sit in his assigned place. The guest of honour responds to this by foaming at the mouth and resisting being seated as if his life depended on it.

There are always a couple of wiseguys at every banquet who believe in buttocks' rights. Their method is to plop down into any chair *except* the seat of honour and declare, 'OK folks, *this* is the seat of honour!' in order to get everyone else to take their places. The other guests are forced to admit defeat, and take their seats, as it were, with their tails between their legs.

On other occasions the fighting continues once the guest of honour finds his place, as the second, third and fourth places of honour must be contested with similar intensity, accompanied by the appropriate yelling and shouting. It often takes ten or twenty minutes before the dust settles, enough time to build up a good appetite. Once the meal begins, there are more skirmishes as the guests try to outdo each other by urging food and drink on the guest of honour.

Rather than go into detail about that here, I'll point out the final battle that takes place after the meal, 'the battle of the doors'. When the banquet is over, the guests get up and head for the door, but instead of simply leaving, they all line up in front of the threshold like penguins terrified of falling into a deep pit full of starving wolves on the other side. The problem is, no one dares be the first to leave, and so another pitched battle ensues. Of course the guest of honour will insist on *not* being the first to go, even at the risk of being dismembered. Finally the mob expels him by brute force, at the same time almost trampling upon the tender heads of those venerables who are less steady on their feet than the rest.

These are just a few of the more obvious examples of the terrifying level to which Chinese 'civilisation' has descended.

Don't act morally, just do what's right

Snobbery is a philosophy of life whose adherents judge things in terms of power and money rather than right and wrong.

A friend of mine told me a story set in his native place in Zhejiang province. During the Japanese occupation, one of his relatives printed up some counterfeit Occupied Territories money to purchase weapons and medicine for the resistance in the occupied areas. But unfortunately the Japanese caught him and shot him just before they surrendered. When the news of his death reached his home village, the village elders said, 'He was a good boy, all right; only problem was, he never behaved properly. If he hadn't started looking for trouble, he wouldn't have ended up this way.' This is how Chinese people feel about people who sacrifice their lives for their country. Though they may have felt sorry about what happened, by saying that he 'never behaved properly', and 'started looking for trouble', they revealed how little respect they had for him.

Such cold-hearted indifference to sacrifice is outright cruelty. In a soy paste vat culture, only seeking fame and fortune is considered proper behaviour. And doing anything that brings neither fame nor fortune is called 'looking for trouble'. This phenomenon can only occur in a culture devoid of humanity and morality, a culture more like a jungle than a civilisation.

Chinatown: a snake pit where Chinese people devour each other alive

Few Chinese ever forget their Chineseness. They never forget to refuse to co-operate with others, nor do they ever forget the art of infighting. Every Chinese community in the world is plagued by bitter infighting.

I understand that an American institute is doing research on Chinese behaviour. One of the topics they are investigating is why Chinese people behave so well in front of non-Chinese Americans, but always seem on the verge of murdering their fellow countrymen. When Chinese youth gangs started to plague Chinese restaurants in the United States, restaurant owners paid huge sums to hire white-skinned guards to sit next to the cash register to ward them off. These guards were as effective as rat poison, and before long the gangs stopped making trouble.

So much for the lowbrow types. Among highbrows, in particular, Chinese academics at American universities, you have a much more refined version of the same mafia-style tactics. One would expect that since they all came from the same place, Chinese academics would be friendly to each other and help each other out. But when I found myself in their midst I realised that you cannot expect very much from Chinese people. Those 'scholarly experts' and 'expert scholars' can talk and write about solidarity in the Chinese academic community with such eloquence that God would cry if he heard their speeches and read their articles. But in real life, these academics behave as if they are living on their own planet.

To cite a few examples: Professor A invited me to dinner at a Chinese restaurant, but insisted that he could not possibly invite Professor B to join us. When Dr C heard I was staying with Professor D, C told me he would never be caught dead in D's presence because he was a terrible snob. When I was leaving Dr E's house, I asked him if he could give me a ride to Professor F's place. Believe it or not, he said, 'You want me to take you there? Better you should walk, the exercise will do you good.'

Chinatowns are infernal machines that swallow Chinese people alive. People working in Chinatowns illegally without US residence permits have little choice but to slave away in sweatshops where they barely earn enough to feed themselves. Like indentured servants, they spend their entire lives in these factories, with no-one to complain to. But even if they had such a sounding board, it is unlikely they would use it. Illegal sewing factories in Chinatown almost exclusively exploit Chinese people. If a white person went to work there the Chinese boss wouldn't dare to rub him or her the wrong way. Chinese people in America who work in the government or in academia treat white people with the same sort of deference.

If you're Chinese and happen to have a Chinese boss, your days are numbered. You can forget about a promotion, and when people are being laid off, you'll be the first to go. But when your Ugly Chinaman boss reports to his white superior about who he has fired, he'll say, 'I'm always fair and impartial'. Actually he's got so much 'partiality' in his brain, you couldn't squeeze it all into the space shuttle. To impress his white boss, an Ugly Chinaman will slaughter one of his compatriots, and then use his corpse as a stepping-stone to further his own career.

Because they suffer from traditional Chinese paranoia, Chinese people are destined to be cheated, abused and taken advantage of from now to the end of time. One Chinese woman in the US who was a victim of a massive swindle told me her sad tale in great detail, but when I said I intended to write about it to help her, she nearly fainted and broke down in tears. 'Bo Yang,' she said, 'you have nothing to fear, since you live in Taipei. And those thugs who robbed me have nothing to fear either. But I have a brother in San Francisco, and so help me God if anything should happen to him, you old, rotten scoundrel . . .' And with that she spat on me, and made me promise that if I wrote about her I would drown myself in a teapot.

Alas! Unlike other people, Chinese are born cowards who lack the courage to think rationally. And those rare individuals who dare to do so are regarded by the grubs festering in the soy paste vat as extremists who don't know their place. Most Chinese muddle through their miserable lives saying, 'Forget about it, let's let bygones be bygones,' and wait around until the Pearly Jade Emperor opens his eyes and publishes a headline like: 'Wicked People Deserve Wicked Punishment'—thereby transforming true heroes who oppose tyranny into 'wicked people'. 'Virtuous people', then, are the worthless, hopeless types, spineless and lacking in individual character, who always end up taking the blame for anything that goes wrong. One reason Chinese youth gangs don't mess around with the white men who sit near the cash register is because they know that while cheating a Chinese is as easy as cheating an ant, dealing with the white man is something entirely different. Chinese people are terrified of any form of confrontation, and thus submit meekly to violence and terror without emitting a peep. But if you make trouble for a white person he'll phone his lawyer and you'll never hear the end of it.

Before I left for the United States, a friend of mine came to say goodbye and said, 'When you get back to Taiwan, I hope we don't have to hear you say "Chinese are the same everywhere".' I tried to control myself, honestly I did, but I finally broke down. Evil old Chineseness, the accumulated dregs of 5000 years of civilisation, is what lies at the root of all Chinese people's troubles. In America's pluralistic society, every Chinese has to stand up for himself, because Chinese people are unable to co-operate with each other. Chinese can achieve a certain degree of influence and respectability in American society, but they always run up against obstacles of their own making. It's obvious that the Chinese will never get ahead of the Jews in America; in fact they're still light years behind the Japanese and the Koreans. There are half as many Japanese as Chinese in the USA, but there are two Japanese–American congressmen. I'm even willing to bet a dollar it'll be 100 years before a Chinese wins an American election.

The American Indian chief Captain Jack once said something that rings painfully true: 'You white people didn't destroy us Indians, we did the damage ourselves'. It isn't white people who have kept the Chinese out of the mainstream in America, it's the Chinese themselves.

A correspondence about 'The Ugly Chinaman'

Dear Bo Yang,
Your article 'The Ugly Chinaman' inspired many thoughts and feelings which I can no longer keep to myself. By setting them down on paper, perhaps I can get them off my mind and provide you with some food for thought.

I thoroughly agree with you that Chinese people need to develop better taste and judgement. But before we produce connoisseurs and learn to discriminate between good and bad, we should first deal with Chinese people's stinginess with praise. Chinese people love to flatter themselves and refer to others as dog shit. The Chinese language is well stocked with illustrious sayings like 'Scholars have little regard for each other', 'People in the same trade always envy each other', and 'People with similar characters repel each other'. Learning to express one's liking or appreciation for things is a good way to begin developing taste and judgement. There's a famous expression, 'The worst kind of enemy is one who has never known kindness'. Chinese people have little tolerance for other people's success. If someone achieves something, they will simply ignore it. If someone does something outstanding, they'll try to subvert it.

I think the reason for this lies in the Chinese habit of never telling the truth. Also, Chinese don't get angry in front of strangers, just as they don't praise people in public. They're incapable of love, and incapable of hate.

This inability to praise others also makes it difficult for Chinese to express gratitude. If a Chinese succeeds in something, he will attribute his success to his own hard work, and overlook the contribution made by the society he lives in or his colleagues. It suffices for him to think he's tops; there is no reason for him to be grateful to society, or to all the people who paved the way for his success. This may partially explain why Chinese lack a sense of social responsibility.

If a Chinese succeeds in something, he will do everything within his power to keep all of the resulting fame and honour within the confines of his own family, group or clan, and prevent outsiders from sharing it. 'My success is none of your business.' 'Your success is none of my business.' Success is an entirely private matter.

Stinginess with praise, a reluctance to get angry, and a tendency to lie and exaggerate can all be related to the basic trend in Chinese culture towards introspection or navel-gazing. Chinese culture has moulded the Chinese personality into an opaque and obscure blob, something which prevents Chinese people from loving, hating, praising, or making sacrifices. (*People don't want to make sacrifices because they know it will only benefit other people.* BY) What's worse, while no one wants to make sacrifices themselves, they expect others to make sacrifices for them. I call this the 'martyr complex'. This vicious circle is the cause of so many problems in China . . .

Sincerely yours,
Chen Wenho

Dear Chen Wenho,
I was moved by your penetrating analysis. You are right in saying that getting a Chinese to say something nice about you is more difficult than pulling teeth. Of course some Chinese people praise others, but only as part of their personal 'diplomacy'. What they say is usually tongue-in-cheek or hypocritical anyway, if it is not some totally unintelligible balderdash, like praising the beauty of a horse's horns. Most Chinese people go through life plagued by a sickening inferiority complex. They can neither perceive nor encourage good things in others; nor can they appreciate the differences between themselves and others. If a Chinese carelessly says something nice about someone, they will suffer the following consequences:

• if the person they are praising enjoys higher status than they do, people will say, 'Oh, there you go licking arse again';

- if the person praised is lower in status, people will say, 'Hey, what are you licking his arse for?';
- if the person praised is a friend or relative, people will say, 'Of course you have good things to say about him, he's your cousin'; and
- if the person praised is a total stranger, people will say, 'You don't even know what he does for a living. If you knew his background, you wouldn't waste your time on him.'

No matter who is the beneficiary, all praise is unacceptable. Only insults and back-stabbing are acceptable, and it is best when it is as casual and natural as dinnertime chitchat. When Chinese get together, if they don't start putting someone down within three minutes, then they aren't bona fide descendants of the Yellow Emperor, the children of the dragon. What is 'the celestial voice of China'? A bunch of vultures getting together and picking at other people's private lives until there's nothing left to pick at. It should be noted that this sort of fault-finding is not necessarily malicious. It's just the virus of Chineseness going through its life cycle.

Every reader must know Mr Dog. Whenever Mr Dog runs into a fellow creature, the two of them will sniff each other's posteriors. If what they discover smells good, both parties will be ecstatic. Chinese people socialise mainly for the purpose of putting other people down. If someone appreciates your insults—in other words, if he or she likes the smell of your posterior—it means the two of you are on the same wavelength.

Lu Xun urged Chinese people to cast off their cowardly ways and be courageous enough to love and hate. Love and hate are two sides of the same coin. Pathologically paranoid Chinese people seem to have lost the ability to love and hate. They are afraid to be made fun of if they love, and are afraid of people avenging them if they hate. After being repressed for years, these feelings of love and hate coalesced into an evil, destructive force which exploded during the Cultural Revolution, China's ten-year holocaust. All the barbarity, violence, duplicity, cunning, resentment and sadism pent up inside Chinese people's hearts was suddenly released. The result was a radical deterioration in the moral fibre of the Chinese people. It will be at least 50 years before the Chinese populace starts engaging in the sort of ethical behaviour that was common in the 1930s. Rebuilding something usually takes five times as long as destroying it.

We should never delegate responsibility for the monumental task of saving a ruined country to the officials of the ruling regime. This responsibility belongs to each and every individual Chinese. A third-rate country can never produce a first-rate government, but many first-rate nations are run by third-rate governments. Saving China begins with you and me. (Of course we can't change China inside out overnight. But if we can do it even one cell at a time, that's fine.)

(from *The Comprehensive Mirror Marketplace*)

False pride

I know many people who get cocky when the subject of the United States comes up. They are fond of saying, 'American culture is so superficial!' Whether American culture is actually superficial is one issue. If it really is superficial, then we ought to be embarrassed about it rather than arrogant. This reminds me of the story of an impoverished descendant of a scholarly family, who is forced by his penury to sleep on a mat in a deserted temple. Yet he still has the gumption to point to a beggar who survives by scrounging leftovers and boast, '*My* grandfather was a prime minister in the Qing dynasty. *His* grandfather cleaned sewers.' Scoundrels of this ilk never ask themselves why they end up where they do, but rather get their kicks from pointing out other people's humble origins. There are many strange things and strange people in this world, and China seems to have a good proportion of them. What that scoundrel said is precisely what other people ought to be saying about China. But if you dare to suggest this, you'll get punched in the nose. Flaunting one's arrogance and calling other people names, as many Chinese are wont to do, is the essence of false pride, and unfortunately it is unlikely that this behaviour pattern will ever disappear.

False pride is simply muddleheaded self-complacency—or call it self-inebriation, mental masturbation, or pulling the wool over one's own eyes. Professor Confucius, PhD, spent many difficult years of his life struggling over the invention he referred to as 'antiquity', and introduced reactionary reforms based on his brainstorm. Today the Ugly Chinaman doesn't have to lift a finger, and the United States of America will appear before his very eyes, a living and breathing entity that he can explore and research and experience. Why do so many Ugly Chinamen have to adopt such a snotty attitude towards this model of a successful nation and hold it in such contempt?

I am not claiming that America is as perfect as a rose. If it were, they wouldn't have to build jails or prisons there. One thing we certainly can emulate is the American lifestyle, a powerful shield the US can use to fend off criticism from overseas students from all over the world: 'You don't like this or that about the US, but can you really criticise the American way of life?' No one can deny that American society is a free and democratic society, as fair and just as any in the world.

False pride is a dead end that leaves us Chinese holed up in a water tank where we become as bloated as Bo Yang's beer-belly, and can no longer absorb anything new, except perhaps some Western guns and battleships. As for the more fundamental aspects of culture, such as education, art, manners, social intercourse and world view, not only is there no room for these things, one glance at them is enough to make the Ugly Chinaman itch uncomfortably all over.

We don't have to copy the US, Germany or Japan. But let us not forget the miraculous recovery achieved by Germany and Japan after World War II. Chinese scholars explain these miracles by citing the Fourth Marshall Plan, the Korean War, and these countries' strong industrial base, as if their success was the result of good luck. These scholars overlook the fact that the Japanese and German economies had been reduced to third-class economies after the war. But both countries had first-class citizens with a strong cultural identity. Imagine a strong man with three heads and six arms fainting and collapsing on the ground, then coming to slowly, knocking the dust off the seat of his pants, standing up and moving on. Then imagine the tubercular Chinaman, strutting about with his nose in the air on the stage of history. A cold wind blows; the Chinaman sneezes three times; his nose starts running; a doctor suggests that he take aspirin; the Chinaman calls the doctor an extremist and accuses him of shaking the foundations of the Chinese state; finally China founders and collapses, and no one can succeed in putting it on its feet again.

Whenever we take after others, a certain loss of face is involved. Every self-respecting country ought to be able to hold up the sky over its own territory with its own two hands, and make all the little fellows jealous by flexing its national biceps. China was able to do this during the Han and Tang dynasties, but times change and fortunes change with the times. The West grew powerful, invincible, unassailable, while China's past greatness faded away like a puff of smoke. Today China's only choice is to learn from the West. But if China persists in showing off her ugly, stinking bound feet and boasting that they are great masterpieces of art, she would do better to choose the path of least resistance, the one which leads directly into Death Valley.

The Ugly Chinaman's sense of false pride arms him with the misconceived notion that China as a nation will never perish. The reason cited is China's ability to absorb and Sinicise other nations. Ah yes, the Mongols conquered us, as did the Manchus, but we turned around and knocked 'em for a loop, we did all right, and sent 'em packing with their tails between their legs. We seem to have given the Manchus a harder time of it: they didn't even have a place to stick their tails. We can bring out these two examples to bolster our self-confidence, but they offer us no guarantee that China will not disappear down the drain of history some time in the future. There's a bit of common sense involved here: no matter how great a nation is, as long as it doesn't disappear off the face of the earth, it can still claim to exist. Similarly, before that nation becomes extinct, it can claim to have had no direct experience of extinction. But when it disappears in the end, it will do so because it has remained aloof and oblivious to obvious threats to its survival both internal and external. And when the threats turn into realities, it is the masses and their descendants who will suffer the most.

When the ancient Greeks first arrived in the Peloponnese, as uncivilised as beasts with their buttocks exposed to the sun, Crete had already attained a high level of civilisation, including such achievements as iron-smelting and some superb works of art. But a mere 200 years later, the Greeks conquered the Cretans and soon the latter were no more. Incan civilisation flourished some 5000 years ago, but where are the Incas today?

I'm not saying all this just to let off steam. We have to realise that the survival of the fittest is something objective. Just because China has racked up 5000 years of history doesn't mean that God is going to send in the troops to protect China from its ultimate dissolution. There is still time for China to get its act together, to purge itself of all poisonous substances (a little laxative now and then wouldn't hurt) and to absorb more nourishment. We now have the luxury of mourning great nations that have become extinct. Let's hope that the people of the future won't have to mourn the demise of China. There's an old saying: 'Don't let our descendants be mourned by their descendants'.

(from *Smashing into the Soy Paste Vat*)

Emulating the West, not becoming its slave

The Annals of Enfeoffed Spirits [*Fengshen yanyi*], China's equivalent of the *Iliad*, is a novel populated with gods, spirits and demons, and while the general theme of the book is the triumph of good over evil, there are some memorable battle scenes. The most despicable monster in the book is called Yin Jiao, who possesses a notorious device called the Earth-crushing Seal. All Yin Jiao has to do is chant a magic spell and shout 'Zap', and the seal shoots up into the air. When it comes down, it destroys whatever it lands on, even objects as big as the Himalaya Mountains. There is a twist in the tale, however. Gao Chengzi, Yin Jiao's master, who taught Yin the secret of the Earth-crushing Seal, is defenceless in the face of his disciple's weapon, and whenever Yin Jiao becomes cross and launches an attack, Gao Chengzi panics and flees.

Everything had been going well for me but suddenly, without warning I became the victim of another sort of hideous weapon of destruction. But since times have changed, this up-to-date, state-of-the-art Earth-crushing Seal goes under a different name and worships another god. Its complete name is 'emulating and having blind faith in the West', or more simply, Xenophilia. If a modern-day Yin Jiao chants a magic spell over Xenophilia, the consequences can be 1000 times more devastating than the after-effects of launching an attack with a 3000-year-old Earth-crushing Seal.

I was lecturing in Los Angeles once when someone in the audience handed me a note which read, 'Old Buddy: I never imagined you would become a Xenophiliac and praise everything in the United States blindly. Actually the USA isn't as great as you think it is.' A few days later, a Chinese newspaper in Los Angeles published an article by a Mr Duo Min, from which I excerpt the following paragraph:

> Xenophilia should be severely criticised. Bo Yang is like the many Chinese who lose their powers of judgement the moment they set foot in the United States, and become enraptured with the idyllic picture that American society presents to the uninitiated. America makes them feel inferior and inadequate, something that soon turns into unseemly self-derogation. If Bo Yang could spend a few years in America, I'm sure he would see the light and revise his opinions about the place.

The all-powerful weapon of Xenophilia was probably invented in the 1840s after the Opium Wars. The inner workings of this omnipotent device can be observed in the rantings of a friend who wrote,

> You Xenomaniacs (*he was being polite; sometimes they're dubbed 'flatterers', 'foreigners' lackeys', or 'foreign collaborators'*) are all the same. In every case, everything American is the best. If you say that the United States is scientifically advanced, I cannot disagree with you. But I refuse to swallow the notion that American culture is superior to Chinese culture. Do you really think we have to live our lives and manage our affairs the way Americans do?

It's not only this old dog who thinks like this. Actually entire packs of them, and even plenty of puppies can be heard barking in this manner. Together they make so much noise, it makes my blood pressure rise.

There's a serious fallacy here: the way people take two entirely unrelated issues and, without using their brains, stick the two together with saliva—high physics indeed! Emulating the West and being a slave of things Western are at least 180 000 miles (288 000 kilometres) apart, but when people stick these two ideas together, the resulting weapon can be used to launch some 'fierce criticism', which can create an incredible amount of trouble. Actually the real victims in this game are not those being attacked as Xenophiliacs, but those who out of fear of being dubbed 'traitors' are reluctant to admit that they admire what is good in the West. I am not suggesting that there aren't people who are both 'traitors' and 'admirers' at the same time; there are enough of them to fill many large baskets. And I can also say that most reasonable people see what is good in the West but don't slavishly worship things Western.

At that gathering in Los Angeles, my tongue declared independence from my brain and I ended up revealing my 'true' nature. Here is a transcription of some of the questions I asked the audience:

> How did you get here from your home tonight, by car or by wheelbarrow? Cars are Western inventions. Why do you part your hair on the side, rather than sport a queue? Parting your hair is a Western fashion. Why don't you women bind your feet, so you can mince about like your grandmother, rather than wear high-heels? Not binding your feet and wearing high-heels is Xenophilic. Why don't you men go to work in long gowns and riding jackets, or wear an oversize gown from the Peking opera, rather than a suit and tie? Why don't you smoke a water pipe, rather than cigarettes? Suits and ties and cigarettes are all Xenophilic. Why don't you cook with coal briquets, wood or wheat stalks, and light the kitchen fire yourself with kindling every night, instead of using gas or electricity? Why don't you sleep on a *kang*, a heated brick bed used by peasants in the North China countryside, instead of on a soft spring mattress? Gas, electricity and spring mattresses are all highly Xenophilic. When you greet your boss, why don't you get down on your knees and bang your head on the floor, rather than shaking hands and saying 'Hi'? Why don't you use oil lamps to read by rather than electric light bulbs? Why do you put stamps on your letters and drop them into a sealed box, rather than entrust a friend to take it to the addressee for you? Why don't you watch hand-operated shadow puppets instead of going to the movies? Why don't you shout all the way across town rather than use the telephone? Although shaking hands, light bulbs, stamps, post

boxes, movies and telephones *are* all Western inventions, I
don't believe a single person here tonight is a Chinese 'traitor'.

When I went back to Taiwan after that, I felt depressed about what I
had said in that talk, and had to clear my conscience in order to prevent
the ghosts from knocking at my door. While Taiwan's National Day
(10 October) ceremonies are still fresh in your mind, let me remind
you of a few things the government likes to show off in the National
Day parade: rifles, cannon, marching drums, bugles, sabres, and military marching bands. These things are all thoroughly foreign, but are
any of them 'traitorous'? When the infantry marches by the reviewing
stand and the air force jets perform a fancy display, the whole show
is directly imported from the West, but is there a hint of collaboration-
ism here?

Peek into the average Chinese home and you'll be startled by what
you see. Everyone who writes articles, books or letters to berate me
for stirring up 'antagonism between the people and the government'
will use a ballpoint pen or a fountain pen, never a Chinese ink brush.
In living rooms, offices and public institutions throughout the country,
how many people sit on hard wooden benches rather than sofas and
armchairs, those symbols of foreign lackeydom?

Last week I was at the house of a friend who called me a Xenomaniac
during our conversation. I was as angry as a raving drunk, picked up
a hammer and was about to smash their modern flush toilet to bits,
when his wife begged me to stop. I swore to her on the spot that I
would never have anything to do with modern flush toilets for the rest
of my life, and once I had finished smashing the toilet, I would start
working on their television set, radio, refrigerator, gas stove, telephone
and every lighting fixture in her home . . .

Finally, their daughter, a college graduate who had been so thoroughly poisoned by Xenophilia that she was entirely lacking in the
traditional Chinese virtues of deference for her superiors and respect
for her elders, called the cops and had me kicked out. If they hadn't
got rid of me and my hammer, they would soon have been deprived
of any place to rest their bare behinds when they most needed it—they
lived on the twelfth floor. Afterwards, I thought about it for a while,
but I couldn't think of any way in which their daughter was acting like
a foreigners' lackey.

I tremble at the thought that God may one day flex his muscles and
in a fit of anger confiscate everything the Chinese have acquired from
the West since they began suffering from Xenophilia. Would there be
anything left? My friends with their Earth-crushing Seals would snort,
'Do you really think we have to live our lives and manage our affairs

the way Americans do?' This guy is about as clearheaded as a paste pot. As for running our lives and affairs, that's where we *really* can learn something from the Western barbarians. But if we do pick up something new from them, does that mean we're licking their barbarian boots?

In the realm of politics, didn't China go head over heels to mimic Western ways, by discarding the 5000-year-old imperial system and adopting the Western electoral system? And didn't China give the system of feudal relationships a kick in the arse and try to replace it with democracy? And how about the way we overturned the Confucian tradition of respect for agriculture and disdain for commerce and put business and industry in the first place? And the way we discarded the ideal of becoming an official as the *sine qua non* for success, and adopted a more diversified social structure? Finally, consider the influence of Western newspapers, television, painting and sculpture, fiction, poetry, drama, music . . . Have all these imported ideas turned China into a nation of Xenomaniacs?

The anthropomorphised Earth-crushing Seal of Xenomania wielded by the likes of my friend Mr Duo Min is a semantic impossibility that defies rational analysis. As Mr Duo wrote, 'If Bo Yang could spend a few years in America, I'm sure he would see the light and revise his opinions about the place'. Of course this *is* a possibility, but there may be other possibilities too. If we want China's military technology to attain international standards, we've got to learn from the West. If we want to improve industrial management, the West can teach us many techniques. If we want to make Chinese society more civil, then we have to take etiquette lessons from the West and learn to say 'please' and 'thank you'. If we want to learn how to form a proper queue, how to cross the street at the pedestrian crossing, and how to prevent others from getting their heads crushed in a spring door, we've got to 'go West'. If we want Chinese to open up their hearts and minds a bit, we have to learn how to offer a helping hand to others with a smile. If we want Chinese to be strong and healthy, we need to do more physical exercise instead of squabbling among ourselves. What does any of this have to do with Xenomania? If we cannot show rudimentary humility in the presence of the manifold achievements of Western civilisation, then we ought to go 'Chinese' whole hog, and keep to our snotty selves. There is an old expression: 'Shame verges upon courage'. If we refuse to admit our faults and weaknesses, all we need to do is throw a temper tantrum, beat our breasts, and rest satisfied that we have done all that there is to do. To admit shame requires both courage and wisdom.

Mr Duo Min supposes that 'feeling inadequate' necessarily leads to 'self-derogation', but these two emotional states are mutually exclusive.

A sense of inadequacy can certainly lead to self-derogating behaviour, but it can also inspire self-knowledge and stimulate self-improvement. This was certainly the Japanese experience during the Meiji Restoration. Being tied up in emotional knots is characteristic of the age of the Earth-crushing Seal, but it's also the essence of Chineseness.

An American professor wrote a book called *Japan as Number One*, but I have never heard of any American calling him a traitor or a Japan-lackey. But when I wrote a few articles based on my superficial impressions of the United States, a whole battery of Earth-crushing Seals were aimed at my head. You can grab me by the neck, but I'll still shout: emulate the West, but don't lick its boots.

(from *Stepping on His Tail*)

Racial prejudice

Racial prejudice is a form of deep-seated hatred that in many places throughout the world is being overcome through the exercise of reason, and by a growing awareness of human rights. But the clever Chinaman, always pompous and judgemental, continues to stew in the juices of emotional provincialism. Perhaps the only solution for us Chinese is to sigh and bemoan our fate.

Chinese people have no right to criticise the racial discrimination practised by white Americans, because the USA probably has the *least* racial discrimination of any country in the world today. If you look at countries, big and small, powerful and weak, the United States seems to be the only country that keeps admitting large numbers of Chinese immigrants every year. And if it weren't for the USA, all those Chinese people whose obsession with emigration verges on insanity would have no place to go. I can't say that white Americans have no overt or covert racial prejudice, or that on some level they don't discriminate against Chinese people. My point is, in addition to old-fashioned racial prejudice, Chinese people practise an even lower form of prejudice—provincial prejudice. In most civilised countries, the concept of provinciality is gradually withering away and being replaced with the interests of one or another political party. Have you ever heard of people from Virginia trying to exclude people from Arizona from their state? Or of the people of Honshu in Japan not accepting people from Kyushu? In fact, racial prejudice in China is much worse than that in America. If you combine exclusivist notions like 'The Descendants of the Yellow Emperor' and Han chauvinism, and add to it such concepts as 'not one of our kind' and 'not of one mind' that are frequently applied to outsiders, people are left with very little room to breathe.

There are Chinese in the USA who have the same social status as American Blacks, but look down on them as if they were dirt. Start talking about Blacks in China, and people will start shaking their heads so hard they are likely to shake them right off. Their condescension is so vicious it's enough to make you choke with anger and die. If eleven per cent of the Chinese population were Black or American Indian, can you imagine how hot-under-the-collar our yellow-faced compatriots would be? People from different parts of China already have a hard enough time getting along with each other. Can you imagine the mess with people of alien races?

Racial prejudice is a problem like ringworm, persistent and widespread but rarely a matter of life and death, so there is no need to expostulate upon it further. What is worth examining is the way it is handled in the United States, and how different this is from the 'Chinese way'. The Chinese method of dealing with racial prejudice is to sweep it under the rug to avoid outside criticism; in other words, to keep their dirty laundry to themselves. Actually this is theoretical, not practical. In practice, Chinese prejudice takes the form of someone bleeding from the rectum, who walks around with both hands covering his backside and proclaiming, 'No, of course I don't have haemorrhoids. Anyone who accuses me of suffering from haemorrhoids has ulterior motives and evil intentions.' These 'ulterior motives' and 'evil intentions' are a powerful traditional cure. All you have to do is say them out loud a few times, and your enemies will run away, while your haemorrhoids will be instantly cured—sorry, that was a slip of the tongue: those haemorrhoids weren't cured, they never existed in the first place. Ugly Chinamen and the grubs that thrive in the soy paste vat spend most of their energy covering their arses. They take pleasure in their haemorrhoids and don't want them cured.

American society is such a strong and healthy organism that it can cure itself of its ailments. When America contracts a case of the piles, instead of covering them up, it goes around telling everyone about them: 'Look, everybody, I've got piles! I'm losing 8000 gallons of blood every day. Give me a price list for coffins!' When everyone hears this news, they all start thinking that they may have haemorrhoids too. People get injections, take medicine and undergo surgery, replace their wooden benches with sofas and armchairs, and stand up straight instead of bending over.

Both the media and popular literature spread information about racial prejudice, so everyone gets scared into thinking that they may be prejudiced themselves. A healthy society rests on the mental health of its citizens. Americans possess the sort of wisdom that allows them to behave in a rational manner, and also the courage and ability to correct their shortcomings. Racial prejudice is a reality, and naturally it is a shortcoming. Americans take logical steps to solve their problems and gradually reduce racial prejudice. Some day, they hope, it will disappear entirely.

Glorious humiliation

At the behest of the Taipei Municipal Board of Education, National Taiwan Normal University carried out a survey of corporal punishment in the Taiwan school system. In their final report, it was revealed that 91 per cent of the teachers, 85 per cent of the parents, and 80 per cent of the students surveyed believed that corporal punishment was appropriate as long as it did not cause physical injury. The survey revealed that both the beater and the beaten, the punisher and the punished, were satisfied with the status quo. At the joint annual conference of the Chinese Psychological Association and the Chinese Psychological Testing Association, a number of scholarly 'hawks' presented papers couched in hocus-pocus academese, in which they proposed that the modern classroom be transformed into the ancient Chinese torture chamber. Then the governor of Taiwan, Lin Yang-kang—whose life story is a mirror image of my own—told the Taiwan parliament that when he was a school boy, he only learned as much as he did because his teachers beat him so hard he had cried out for his mother. Liu Chia-yu of the National Yangming Medical School also made a recommendation to the Ministry of Education that teachers should apply corporal punishment as necessary.

But the first prize for the best contribution on the subject should go to a Ms Yang Shu-hui of the *Independent Evening News*, who began her article on the subject with the headline:

> Love or corporal punishment?
> The question is a matter of appropriateness. If we want to prevent students from going astray, the Board of Education does not need to set strict limits on corporal punishment.

Her article contained a few immortal lines that deserve to be quoted here (comments in brackets by Bo Yang):

> A certain male teacher in one of Taipei's leading middle schools was renowned for his 'teaching whips' as well his 'teaching results'. On the first day of class, he hung up a number of rattan strips in a prominent place in the classroom. (*Just like an old-fashioned torture chamber.*) He made a deal with his students: for every point they scored on their examinations below the average, they would receive so many

lashings. As a result, all the students in his classes got very high marks. (*Very few of them were not promoted.*) He was one of the best-known teachers in the school. (*Had he displayed a steel executioner's sword in the classroom, his fame might have spread to London.*) Every student wanted to take his classes. (*We need some numbers here, not a generalisation like this.*) After they graduated, many of his former students reported that they missed 'lining up and having their palms beaten'. (*Maybe they felt like this immediately after taking Taiwan's gruelling unified university entrance examinations, but I doubt if this nostalgia would last much after that.*) This suggests that the question is not whether we should institute corporal punishment or not (*though for the teacher this is critical*), but rather the *importance* of corporal punishment in education.

This article is one of those unique by-products of the soy paste vat culture. In fact, this by-product was already 'on the market' in China back in 1068, during the Song dynasty. In those days, it was the practice of the Chinese emperor to remain seated while listening to the lectures of his tutor, who like an attendant would stand at the emperor's side. Then the prime minister and the imperial tutor Wang Anshi made the bold suggestion that the tutor should also be allowed to sit down. When the news of Wang's suggestion spread through the court, the soy paste vat began to bubble. One of the grub-faced ministers of the day, Lu Hui, reacted as if someone had stepped on his grubby grub's tail and called for Wang Anshi's impeachment:

> Wang Anshi embraces the vain hope of remaining seated when he tutors the emperor. This would cause the emperor to sacrifice his dignity, and constitute an elevation in the status and dignity of the imperial tutor. Wang has no regard for the harmonious relationship between inferiors and superiors, and ignores the proper distinction between monarch and subject.

How pitiful that in olden times, there were teachers who actually took pride in standing at the emperor's side while teaching, the same way that students today think it is proper to 'line up to get their palms whipped'. I recall an incident that took place in the 1910s, not long after the founding of the Republic of China. A Manchu loyalist appeared before the entrance of a prefectural government office, bared his buttocks, and had one of his relatives beat him with a paddle. While this was taking place, he cried out in joyous pain: 'Ah, wonderful, wonderful, it's been years since I enjoyed a good beating!' This sort of display is even more 'progressive' than having your palms beaten.

I am befuddled by the way Chinese people cannot relinquish the slave mentality. Three of the cruellest and most inhumane inventions of Chinese culture—bound feet, eunuchs and corporal punishment for crimes—are now obsolete. The Municipal Board of Education's decision to forbid corporal punishment in the classroom is one of the only admirable decisions it has ever made; it is hard to believe that in the 1980s there are many people who wish to challenge it. The problem is, humiliation is humiliation. Only people who are hopelessly trapped in the slave mentality can perform the miracle of transforming something so obviously humiliating into something glorious and honourable. There is nothing remarkable about the existence of scholarly 'hawks'. What is remarkable is that there are so many young people like Lu Hui willing to line up and have their palms beaten. They constitute a serious threat to the survival of the Chinese nation. If this sort of humiliating behaviour can be construed as honourable, then there is no real honour left in this world. People who enjoy being humiliated are either entirely insensitive to normal human feelings or are acting under the pretence of appearing not to care, but actually harbour malicious intentions. Or perhaps they are simply born slaves or slaves in the making.

The 'hawks' make the point that if there is 'love' behind corporal punishment, there is nothing wrong with it. Alas! How many crimes are committed every day in the name of 'love'? Parents bound their daughters' feet to ensure that they would be able to find husbands. Paternalistic rulers beat their subjects until their flesh dripped with blood as part of a policy of 'using no corporal punishment during the term of imprisonment'. This raises a question: if a teacher beats a student once, is this 'love'? If he beats the student ten or 100 times, is this 'love'? If a teacher gives a student a concussion when he whacks him in the head three times, and the teacher insists he is acting out of concern for the student, then where do you draw the line? And how do you judge what is right and wrong? In the textbook of education through 'love', you will never find a chapter devoted to torture. How much punishment is 'appropriate'? Who will set the standards, and how do we judge if they are being met? Although teachers are supposed to avoid causing 'physical harm' to their students, doesn't all corporal punishment cause some physical harm? Is there any sense in saying, put your hand in the oven for as long as you can, just as long as it doesn't cause any physical harm? About as much sense as in a leaky balloon.

When a teacher is about to beat a student, he usually flexes his muscles and his eyes bulge in their sockets. The hideous expression on his face and the hostile look in his eyes can in themselves be harmful to the student. Consider also the humiliation the student feels when confronted with the teacher's absolute authority, the same effect a father has on his child when he raises his arm threatening a spanking. Clearly there is no love here, only the seeds of mutual hate, and an affront to human dignity.

When students lose their enthusiasm for lining up to be beaten, they will also rid themselves of their sense of shame, and corporal punishment will lose its effectiveness. If students who fail to come up to certain standards on examinations are subject to violent punishment and oppression, they will soon lose their self-esteem, their intelligence and their creativity. On the other hand, when the Ministry of Education bans corporal punishment in the classroom, will 92 per cent of all teachers 'lose their enthusiasm for their work, and become lax in their teaching'? If educated people hired by the government as teachers feel their hands are tied because they can no longer beat their students until they squirm with pain, and as a result become slack in their work, the Ministry of Education should have the right to fire them and offer them jobs as bodyguards at gambling casinos.

I lack the resources to oppose the vast majority of teachers, parents and students who approve of corporal punishment. But I want to offer one personal suggestion to all those students suffering abuse and insults from their teachers' whipping. If they ever hit you, though you cannot retaliate now, you can, like a grown-up, swear to take your revenge in the future—ten years hence is certainly not too late. Some particularly vicious teachers may swear at you as they lay on the whip, 'Take this! Take this! I'll be waiting for you in ten years!' You ought to mark snakes of this sort, and make a point of getting back at them when you are ten years older.

But this is not my main point. What is so shocking and depressing is the fact that such a high percentage of people in Taiwan approved of beating and being beaten when they were surveyed. The purpose of education is to develop the individual's sense of dignity and self-respect. But it seems that a majority of those involved in the business of education, both students and teachers, seem to agree that the true purpose of education is to destroy the dignity of the young. This has to be one of the most shocking educational scandals in the twentieth century. It also suggests the great depth of the soy paste vat, and the thickness of the sauce inside. Finally it demonstrates how perverted the educational system has become: education has become anti-education. Whenever I think of it, I shudder.

(from *Stepping on His Tail*)

PART III
Waves breaking on the shore: an Ugly Chinaman forum

Are Chinamen so ugly?

Sun Guodong, *Guangming Daily* (Beijing),
1 March 1987

When I read *The History of the Han Dynasty* several years ago, I particulary admired the way Xia Housheng and Huang Ba risked punishment for daring to criticise the emperor in their writings. When I learned many years ago that Bo Yang been been arrested for something he had written, and that he had read many books about Chinese history and written much while he was in jail, I naturally assumed that Bo Yang shared many qualities with Xia and Huang, and developed a strong feeling of admiration for him. But because I was so busy with my work, I never got around to reading anything he had written. Not long ago I had an opportunity to acquire a copy of the ninth printing of Bo Yang's book, *The Ugly Chinaman*, published by the Linbai Publishing Company in Taipei, which contained the texts of several speeches Bo Yang gave in various universities in the United States and selections from his essays. I devoured the book in a single sitting; it left me feeling as if I had a bone stuck in my throat that I had to spit out, so I wrote the following to share with Bo Yang.

I

Bo Yang blames all of the despicable conduct of the Chinese people today on the 'poisonous' influence of 5000 years of Chinese culture. This is pure exaggeration. Let us examine Bo Yang's evidence. In the speech he gave at the University of Iowa, he said:

> Chinese culture is infected with a virus which has been passed down from generation to generation, and which today still resists cure. There is an old saying: 'If you are a failure, you

101

can blame your ancestors'. But there is a significant flaw in this argument. In Ibsen's play *Ghosts,* a syphilitic couple give birth to a syphilitic son, who has to take medicine every time his illness flares up. At one point in the drama, the son exclaims, 'I never asked you for life. And what sort of a life have you given me?' In all fairness, can we blame the son, and not blame his parents?

Based on this premise, Bo Yang concludes that responsibility for all the troubles of China today can be laid at the door of traditional culture, and that 5000 years of Chinese culture and history are the source of all sorts of evil-doing. Actually, it is Bo Yang's logic that is seriously flawed. It is true that the son in *Ghosts* is suffering from an illness transmitted to him by his parents. The real question is, did his parents inherit their syphilis from their ancestors, or did they get the clap from engaging in illicit sexual relations? If their ancestors had caught syphilis 5000 years ago, then their family line would have died out long ago. We can only blame the son's suffering on the sins of his parents, and not on his ancestors. Likewise we should not blame China's present-day problems on our ancient ancestors, but rather on the failure of our more immediate ancestors—our parents, grandparents and great-grandparents—to have taken steps to improve China.

Not only does Bo Yang use flawed logic to explain the present crisis of Chinese culture, he also denigrates the constructive influence that the Confucians have had on Chinese culture throughout history. He wrote:

> The Confucians seemed to have two lofty aspirations: the first was to teach the common people to keep their heads stuck in the sand, their tails tucked between their legs, and their noses out of politics. The masses were encouraged to devote the bulk of their energy protecting their families and their property . . .
> The second aspiration was to try to encourage those in power to show mercy to the helpless common people, and to beseech officials to take pity on them and go easy when trampling on their heads.
> . . . It is a tragedy for China that in all the Confucian teachings, there is little encouragement for intelligent thinking, scarce mention of the responsibility incumbent upon people in authority, and almost no stimulus for competition. Confucius only wanted his disciples, and his disciples' disciples, to accept the status quo, and to remain smug and self-satisfied. You could act as you pleased, as long as you never took risks.

These two passages reveal Bo Yang as ignorant, slanderous and downright insulting. Two major trends in philosophy emerged during the heyday of the pre-Qin thinkers. One was the Confucian school, promoting active social engagement, which took 'benevolence' and 'righteousness' as its ideals. The other was the school of Laozi (Lao Tzu) and Yang Zhu, representing the more passive and reclusive side of human existence. The Taoists taught people to be guided in their action by natural phenomena, and made the integration of body and mind and the preservation of life its highest goals. Both of these schools had a profound influence on Chinese society.

The message of the Confucians was relatively straightforward. The *Analects* of Confucius contains such statements as:

- The determined scholar and man of virtue will not seek to live at the expense of injuring their virtue. They will even sacrifice their lives to preserve their virtue complete.
- To see what is right and not to do it is want of courage.
- The commander of the forces of a large state may be carried off, but the will of even a common man cannot be taken from him.

Do these teachings have anything to do with 'keeping their heads stuck in the sand and their tails tucked between their legs'? Are they totally devoid of 'intelligent thinking'? Throughout Chinese history, the great majority of men who sacrificed their lives for righteous, patriotic causes were Confucian scholars. In the *Twenty-four Dynastic Histories* you will find the names of more than 1000 men who died for honourable causes. Most of these were men educated in the Confucian tradition. And an even greater number of those mentioned in the pages of the 'Biographies of Men of Benevolence and Righteousness', the 'Biographies of Men of Integrity' and the 'Biographies of Men of Sincerity'—all of whom gave up their lives for what they believed in—were adherents of the Confucian school.

There are many examples of collective opposition to the abuse of authority that display the spirit of Confucianism. First we can cite Li Ying and Chen Fan, who led a number of scholars from the Imperial Academy in a struggle against corrupt eunuchs during the Eastern Han dynasty, as a result of which the entire scholarly faction was nearly wiped out; and then there was the late-Ming Donglin clique, who also engaged in a bloody conflict with the eunuchs. Is this 'keeping their noses out of politics'? Is this 'doing anything you please, as long as you never take risks'? Bo Yang lards his writings with old clichés like 'In books one finds golden palaces, and beautiful women with complexions as fine as jade' as a way of casting aspersions on the Confucians. Writing in the guise of a historian, Bo Yang fabricates his evidence and engages in intellectual deception.

The Confucians stress 'benevolence' and 'righteousness', but Bo

Yang says, ' "Benevolence" is nothing but the pity and sympathy shown to the common people by the ruling class. The ruling class dispenses benevolence as if it were a charitable donation or a personal favour, or as a way of displaying their generosity, similar to the way kindergarten teachers treat their charges.' But Confucian 'benevolence' is based on real human feelings and finds expression in benevolent acts. Note the following Confucian beliefs: 'A compassionate mind exemplifies perfect benevolence'; 'Only a man of benevolence can truly love and hate others'; and 'Fine words and an insinuating appearance are seldom associated with benevolence'.

In these statements, 'benevolence' grows out of feelings that are strictly personal. Why must the practice of 'benevolence' be limited to those in power? And what does authentic 'benevolence' have to do with charity?

Bo Yang has also written:

> The teachings of Dr Mencius can be summed up in his famous line: 'How can you speak of benefit? There is only benevolence and righteousness.' Here the old moraliser is handing out masks of 'benevolence' and 'righteousness' to the ten billion grubs that inhabit the soy paste vat. All these grubs are obviously suffering from tertiary syphilis, with their noses rotting away, so they don their Confucian masks and say, 'Hey, everybody, come and look. See how pretty I am!'

Can you imagine anything more crude, vile and vulgar! Why should teaching people to ignore their own private interests and cultivate such virtues as benevolence and righteousness be interpreted as providing future generations with masks to cover their syphilitic sores and diseased noses? Earlier Bo Yang had calumniated the Confucians for having taught people to '. . . ignore politics and devote the bulk of their energy to protecting their families and their property'. Yet here he is again attacking Mencius for being concerned with benevolence and righteousness, and for eschewing personal benefit. Bo Yang is only proving that his thinking is hopelessly confused and self-contradictory.

II

Bo Yang wrote:

> When I was in Los Angeles a few years ago, someone asked me, 'What do Chinese people have to be proud of?' I answered, 'I'm not at all proud to be Chinese. You tell *me* what Chinese people should be proud of! A powerful country? A great culture? Our contributions to civilisation? Great music,

painting and literature? Is there anything we can really be proud of? Show me something that is uniquely Chinese, something that no other civilisation possesses, or something that we share with another country that we can feel proud about.

Have you ever heard anyone ask so many shocking questions? It is true that over the course of the last hundred years or so, China's achievements in the social and natural sciences have fallen behind those of the West. But if we start to compare Chinese achievements in literature, history, art and philosophy, there is certainly much room for argument. My wife is doing research on the Mao edition of the *Book of Songs*. It is astounding to think that the living pulse of works of literature written 3000 years ago still beats in the literature of the present day. We even find lines from the *Book of Songs* in our daily speech:

> At first when we set out,
> The willows were fresh and green.

> One day without seeing him,
> Is like three autumns.

> There is a young lady embracing thoughts of spring
> And a fine gentleman who would lead her astray.

The *Book of Songs* is full of many such memorable lines. What country in the world can boast of works of literature penned 3000 years ago that still seem fresh today?

I have a modest understanding of history, and a thorough comparison of Chinese and Western history would be too complex an undertaking to attempt here. The basis of written history is the systematic recording of events. In this respect alone, Chinese historical writing is far superior to that of the West. Leaving aside the works of the pre-Zhou (eleventh century BC to 221 BC) historians, historical annals were first compiled in China beginning in the year 841 BC, in the Zhou dynasty. And from 206 BC (the first year of the reign of Emperor Gaodi of the Han dynasty) we have formal chronicles of major events. In other words, China has a detailed written history that dates back 2800 years. Can any other nation in the world claim to possess such an extended continuous history? An investigation into the enduring qualities of Chinese literature and history may provide us with some clues to the remarkable continuity of Chinese civilisation.

III

Bo Yang's discussions are often filled with exaggerations and contradictions. When he addressed a group of Chinese students studying in the United States, he praised the Chinese people for their high intelligence. But elsewhere he wrote: 'Scholars were not permitted to think independently, because everything had been thought out for them. Thus they became uncreative and unimaginative, and were incapable of making critical judgements.'

If Chinese scholars are uncreative, unimaginative and unable to make critical judgements, why don't *all* the Chinese students studying in the United States have low IQs? Can Chinese people with their low IQs, the result of 2000 years of accumulated debilities, raise their IQs simply by setting foot on American soil? It is obvious that everything Bo Yang says about Chinese people being uncreative, unimaginative and unable to make judgements is pure rubbish.

Bo Yang has a lot of good things to say about the Opium Wars:

> Maybe we Chinese should be grateful for the Opium Wars. Where would China be today without them? . . . If the Opium Wars had taken place 300 years earlier than they did, China might have had a head start on modernisation, and if they had taken place 1000 years ago Chinese history would be unimaginably different.

Bo Yang's attributing reform in China to the influence of the Opium Wars is certainly plausible, but is he aware that if we 'rescheduled' the Opium Wars 1000 years earlier, to the ninth century, this would place them smack in the middle of the illustrious Tang dynasty, when Europe was still groping its way through the Dark Ages? During this period all the major nations of Asia sent scholars to China to study. In the seventeenth and eighteenth centuries Chinese philosophy had an influence on the European Enlightenment. Why does Bo Yang wish that the Opium Wars had taken place in the ninth century? There is only one possible explanation: Bo Yang believes incorrectly that the last thousand years of Chinese history have been a Chinese Dark Ages, while the last millennium in the West has been nothing but glorious achievements and progress. Bo Yang insists that he only worships the West, but doesn't lick its boots. Isn't this a perfect example of bootlicking?

IV

The remarks above spring from my numerous doubts about the nonsensical and irresponsible way in which Bo Yang disparages Chinese culture. Bo Yang himself has written, quite correctly, that 'self-examination is the first step towards progress'.

Self-examination may be easy for an individual, but it is difficult for an entire nation. For a nation to attain self-awareness there are several preconditions: first, every individual must have love and appreciation for his own nation. Without this love any real self-searching is impossible.

Secondly, every individual must understand his nation's history and culture. Without such an understanding, any self-examination will only result in specious conclusions. Much scholarship is required to trace the original flaws in a culture with a 5000-year-long history. One must consider such factors as politics, economy, society, philosophy, the family, religion, scholastic thought, geography and foreign relations.

Thirdly, any national self-examination must be carried out according to the laws of reason, without indulging in emotionalism. Even a single emotional outburst can fog a clear-thinking mind. A national self-examination should not merely seek to identify the source of all the unhealthy tendencies plaguing China, but rather pursue a national mission, and the major forces that can contribute to national survival. From reading *The Ugly Chinaman*, it is evident that Bo Yang's understanding of Chinese culture is superficial. Through groundless and irrational vilification, Bo Yang completely discredits Chinese culture, and obliterates any love that Chinese people may have for their nation. Has Bo Yang examined himself? Can he inspire the Chinese people to examine themselves? I feel that people who read Bo Yang's essays may have two rather extreme reactions: the first is to feel shame about being Chinese, and to distance oneself from the Chinese people; the second is to conclude that every line Bo Yang has written is an overstated lie, and adopt the general attitude that the Chinese people have no faults or shortcomings and can do no wrong. Both of these attitudes are dangerous and potentially damaging to China. This is why I believe that *The Ugly Chinaman* has more of a negative than a positive influence on reform in China.

No one can deny that Chinese culture has its shortcomings. Is there such a thing as a 'perfect' national culture? For the last few hundred years, China has been the 'sick man of Asia'. But no nation in the history of the world has thrived forever. We have no right to disparage Chinese culture as something irredeemably evil, simply because it has deficiencies and because the Chinese people as a whole are 'sick'. Since the birth of civilisation six or seven thousand years ago, countless nations have risen and fallen, and some have disappeared entirely. Yet the Chinese people have survived. This suggests that despite all its flaws, Chinese culture has a remarkable inner strength that has sustained it over the millennia.

Chinese people today certainly have their ugly side; but they have a lovable side as well. If Bo Yang sincerely wants the Chinese people to improve their lot, he would do well to refrain from destroying the love that the Chinese people have for their nation. I would also like to remind Bo Yang that there are similarities between the biology of culture and the biology of organisms: only by absorbing and digesting rich nourishment can a culture, like an organism, grow strong and healthy. Sever the roots of this organism or culture, however, and no nourishment, regardless of how rich it is, can be of any use to it.

I am a humble educator. For the last 30 years, I have taught Chinese students on the primary, middle, university and post-graduate level. My experience in education has taught me that in order to get young people to learn and improve themselves, we must not only point out their shortcomings in a straightforward and unexaggerated way, we must also do everything we can to nourish their self-esteem and self-confidence. If we injure young people's sense of self-esteem and self-respect, they are bound to resign themselves to failure. Bo Yang ignores the realities of life, and mercilessly attacks Chinese people's sense of self-esteem and self-confidence. Does Bo Yang really want the Chinese people to improve themselves? Or does he want them to be resigned to living on the trash heap of history?

The soy paste vat: symbol of all that is wrong with Chinese culture

Yao Limin, *The Seventies Magazine* (Hong Kong), November/December, 1984

When we compare the strength and wealth of Japan and the United States with the poverty and weakness of China today, we can only ask one question: How has this come about?

There are two ways possible answers. First, the Chinese people are stupid. And second, traditional Chinese culture is seriously flawed.

There are two ways to look at the first answer. Firstly, Chinese people are indeed stupid. Perhaps they are a bit brighter than the ancient Huns and Turks and Africans today (*this may change in the future* BY), but certainly less clever than the Americans, English, Germans, Russians and Japanese. And secondly, our ancestors were pretty smart operators; at least they deserve credit for the greatness of the Han and Tang dynasties. But their IQs declined with each succeeding generation, and after a few more centuries go by, China will turn into a nation of imbeciles.

If our national intelligence is really to blame, then we must accept this as a fact and ask who is at fault for the Chinese people having fallen so far behind the rest of the world. According to the theory of the 'survival of the fittest', any country that turns into a 'third-rate colonial power' deserves that fate. Put in another way, if the problem lies with Chinese culture rather than Chinese brains, then China still has a splendid future, but we first need to examine ourselves carefully and to rid ourselves of our cultural burden.

The issue of Chinese intelligence mentioned above is purely theoretical, because there isn't a single Chinese alive today who will admit that the Chinese mind is inferior. This denial is not subjective, emotional, or self-aggrandising, but rather entirely rational and demonstrable. What evidence do the Chinese have to back up this assertion?

Firstly, the fact that most of the wealth in Southeast Asia was created by the Overseas Chinese; and secondly, the outstanding academic achievements of the Chinese in America. Even white people with their feelings of superiority have to admit that individual Chinese are extraordinarily intelligent. But they also know that Chinese people do not work well with one another, lack the instinct for co-operation, fight bitterly among themselves, and are unable to exert any influence as a group.

In one of Bo Yang's essays, there is a Buddhist tale in which a monk says:

> If you wish to learn about your former life,
> Your present life embodies it.
> If you wish to learn about your future life,
> Your present life creates it.

Bo Yang quotes this little verse in order to teach us something about China's 5000-year-old culture. To judge this culture, we don't have to bury our heads in a mountain of ancient books. We only have to open our eyes and note the hardships that the Chinese are enduring today. We have raised the question, and provided a tentative answer—Chinese culture is flawed. We must now analyse this further.

In his 'Environment and Cultural Soil', Sun Kuan-han, one of Bo Yang's great admirers, wrote:

> The reason why China cannot become a sane and happy country has nothing to do with any inherent characteristics of the Chinese people, but rather with their 'acquired characteristics'. Simply stated, this is a question of environment, not inheritance. As a farmer would say, the problem lies with the soil, not the seeds. The soil is affected by such factors as nutrients, water, air, and sunlight. When we talk about a nation, 'the soil' means the social environment, including human customs and habits. It is a fact that throughout history, China has never produced a healthy 'social plant species'. If the problem does not lie with the seeds we have planted, then we must admit that some areas of our 'soil' or environment are not suitable for cultivation . . . I am now convinced that our 5000-year-old corpus of culture and customs has a number of flaws in it, as well as many good things. The bad part is the environment in which good seeds cannot flourish. This vast and terrible concatenation of Chinese culture and customs is what Bo Yang refers to, specifically and generally, as the 'soy paste vat'.

What is the soy paste vat, and what's inside it? Bo Yang's own definition is, 'A chaotic society riddled with corruption and stultification, a society racked by the politics of enslavement, perverse morality, an overly self-centred world view, and the worship of power and money, a society where normal human intelligence has become so ossified that little of it remains intact'. Bo Yang also says that the various ingredients of the soy paste vat have combined to produce 'irrational worship of authority', 'overbearing selfishness', 'deceptive language', 'an infatuation with corpses', 'an inability to co-operate', 'cold and heartless jealousy and cruelty', and 'arrogance and carelessness'.

Before discussing the products of the soy paste vat, I want to mention a few other things, because once I start with the soy paste vat, I am sure I won't allow myself to get a word in edgewise.

Some patriotic Chinese think that China must become a rich and powerful country—there is no other way out. What matters here is *how* China will become rich and powerful. Shall we accomplish this by showing off our ancestors' scars? Is there any use in blaming everything on our ancestors? And if we do blame them until there is nothing left to blame, will that prevent China from becoming rich and powerful?

I don't agree with this approach. The Chinese people, as a nation, are indeed 'sick', and as time goes by they grow sicker and sicker. The sickness started back in the Han dynasty with the Martial Emperor, who adopted Confucianism as the state philosophy. This sickness got sicker when a few odball ideas (like the examination system and the Neo-Confucianism of the Song and Ming dynasties), took over the place, knocked all the intelligence out of the Chinese people, and left them gasping for breath. China's early adversaries, such as the Xiongnu, Turks, Khitans and Xixia, had such flimsy cultural identities that they could not resist Sinification. Even the Mongols and Manchus, who conquered China by virtue of their superior military prowess, were in the end conquered by Chinese culture. These successive cultural victories allowed us to ignore, or remain ignorant of, our own 'illness'. Finally, the Qing dynasty opened the doors of the empire to the West. These unprecedented adversaries, the 'new barbarians', who took us completely by surprise, exposed all of our flaws and turned us into basket cases.

Like a sick person, if a basket-case culture doesn't get well, it is useless to talk of any positive accomplishments. Democracy and science are excellent tonics, but what is the use of feeding a tonic to a patient with a severe case of gastroenteritis? To cure an illness, it is essential to know its cause. The patient cannot pretend to be well, nor shrink from a possibly painful cure. If necessary, the patient must be prepared to undergo amputation or even a transplant operation. Only if he is courageous enough to undergo such radical procedures is there any hope of recovery. This explains the importance of carrying out an open-minded self-examination of the chronic symptoms from which Chinese traditional culture suffers.

Numerous scholars have pointed out that the Chinese nation is sick, but have they prescribed the proper medicine? If you read between the lines, the cure consists of listing the symptoms one by one, investigating the precise cause of each of them, and then urging each thinking Chinese person to examine these symptoms within themselves. If the symptoms persist, do something to remedy them; if not, enjoy your good health while it lasts. If more people do this sort of thing, China will eventually cure itself, without drugs. Of course this is easier said than done, but we shall not go into that here.

On the subject of Chinese indifference to suffering, cruelty and envy, we might refer to an incident recorded by Miss Zhu Xiujuan in her book, *My Experiences in New York*. When Miss Zhu first arrived in New York, she was strolling around with her husband one day, when they ran into a Chinese man. Experiencing the joy of 'meeting an old friend in a faraway place', she greeted him warmly, but he ignored her completely. Unwilling to accept defeat, she consoled herself by saying, 'He must be Japanese'. Ten minutes later, they ran into the same person on the subway train, and noticed that he was reading a Chinese martial arts novel. Her conclusion was, 'He must have thought *we* were Japanese'. Although this seems like an obvious conclusion, I found it rather depressing. Is this what Bo Yang means by Chinese indifference and cruelty?

How to correct the habit of being perfect

Editorial, *Huayu Express* (New York), 12
August 1981

In his recent speech in New York, the Taiwanese writer Bo Yang suggested that the reason why Chinese people seem to be unable to improve themselves is because of their stubborn resistance to admitting their mistakes. While this is a commonplace observation and hardly original, it is still penetrating and convincing. Bo Yang raises the question of whether the flawed and destructive policies carried out by the Chinese government over the last several decades, and its stubborn clinging to the same worthless political ideology, are the result of an inability to admit errors. Although Bo Yang fails to hit the nail on the head, he is not far from the mark.

If we delve a bit deeper, we are bound to discover that face-saving and a reluctance to admit errors are universal human foibles. A passage in the New Testament talks about how everyone has two pockets, a front pocket where we keep other people's shortcomings, and a rear pocket where we keep our own shortcomings. This is to suggest that people prefer to find fault with others rather than own up to their own weaknesses. The Bible tells us that this habit was prevalent as early as 2000 years ago, and not only in China.

If the inability to admit errors is universal, then how has the West made such stunning progress in the realm of politics, economics, culture and science, while China remains stuck in the mud of backwardness? Is there some contradiction here? The answer lies in the political system. If everyone has two pockets, the front pocket full of others' shortcomings and the rear pocket full of our own shortcomings, then we ought to remove the contents of our rear pockets and put them in other people's front pockets, to enable us to see them more clearly. And if everyone opens up their front pockets, the original contents of all the back pockets will be exposed to public scrutiny; it will be impossible to hide or deny anything. This is otherwise known as 'freedom of speech' and 'democracy', the most effective known medicines for curing the illness of not admitting error. On the other hand, where there is no democracy, the rulers can seal the mouths of the ruled. The rulers can only see as far as their own front pockets, while the pockets of the ruled are sealed and inaccessible. Thus the errors of the rulers never see the light of day and are never rectified. The country deteriorates, and when the dynasty collapses the rulers bring devastation upon the the entire society.

Do Western countries make similar mistakes? Of course they do, and many of their mistakes are serious, for instance, the exploitation of labourers during the early days of capitalism, and the oppression of colonised people by imperialism. But because the imperialists were basically democratic, they did not stop people from speaking out. Remember that Karl Marx held the first international meeting of the communist party in London. In a free and democratic society, the government's errors and omissions are constantly exposed to public scrutiny and improvements are made. The parliament was established and laws were passed to protect labourers, whose lives improved markedly. One positive outcome of the two world wars was the fact that many colonies gained their independence.

Confucius praised the mythological emperor Yu by saying, 'When he learned of his errors he was pleased'. Confucius also said, 'The errors of the sage are like the passage of the sun and moon through the heavens', but he noted that ordinary people like to cover up their shortcomings. Confucius wanted everyone to be a sage, but he failed to develop a practical method of accomplishing this. The West found a solution in the democratic system, which elevates every elected official to quasi-sagehood—at least in regard to making mistakes. The behaviour of Western politicians is like 'the passage of the sun and moon through the heavens', everyone can watch them with their own eyes. If they do something wrong and don't change their ways, they're out. Certainly there is no more effective system of rule. In sum, if we want every individual to acknowledge his faults (we can hardly expect everyone to become a sage), the only way to accomplish this is through democracy, which makes it impossible for those in power to conceal their wrongdoing.

Reasoning gone wrong

Editorial, *China Express* (New York),
13 August 1981

In our editorial yesterday we commented on Bo Yang's speech in which he spoke of Chinese people's habit of denying their shortcomings and faults. We suggested that in order to correct this pervasive bad habit in our culture, we could not depend on individuals achieving sudden enlightenment and showing repentance for their misdoings of their own free will. To embrace such a hope is to assume that 'all people are sages like Yao and Shun', which is daydreaming that leads nowhere. The only remedy for China's ills is to change the present political system, and by so doing exert pressure on people who are unwilling to change in order to ensure that they *will* change.

When discussing Chinese people's faults, we were reminded that Chinese people's ability to think logically is significantly inferior to that of Western people. Every nationality has its own particular strengths and weaknesses. For example, Chinese people are undoubtedly the most intuitive people on earth. This is evident from the fact that the Chinese invented the compass and gunpowder many centuries before they appeared in Europe. But the Chinese never developed theoretical science: they could make compasses and gunpowder, but they did not understand how they worked. In fact the science of logic was never developed in China, while by the time of Aristotle, logic was understood and used as a tool of reasoning in Greece. This suggests that the Chinese are a bit backward when it comes to logic.

Bo Yang says that Chinese people refuse to admit their errors, but in fact Chinese people were aware of the importance of this in ancient times. More than 2000 years ago, Confucius said, 'There is no greater good than being able to correct one's errors'. But Confucius' way of doing this was to get people to emulate the mythological sages of yore,

Yao and Shun. This is purely subjective and intuitive. Of course it would be marvellous if everyone could be as painfully honest as Yao and Shun, but this is impossible. Actually, following this method is like following no method at all, and although this sort of emulation has been taught for the last 2000 years, no-one has matched the integrity of Yao or Shun.

If the Chinese people were capable of logical reasoning, they would have invented democracy a long time ago, and made use of the freedom of speech to correct the errors of their rulers. The Watergate affair that led to Richard Nixon's resignation is a perfect example of the democratic process at work. On the other hand, it took the Chinese government several years to announce the number of people that died in the 1976 Tangshan earthquake. Millions died in China during the ten-year rule of the Gang of Four, and if the illustrious quartet hadn't been jailed, we might still believe that Chairman Mao's theory of 'endless struggle' could create heaven on earth. Is there any doubt that without democracy, there is no truth, and no righting of wrongs?

Even today, many Chinese people trust that their leaders will act like Yao and Shun, and don't insist on having a system of checks and balances, or even freedom of speech. Doesn't this prove that Chinese people cannot think straight? Despots hate democracy because it deprives them of their privileges. It is quite strange how people in China shout: 'Western democracy is bourgeois democracy, Western democracy is reactionary'. Those who shout such slogans seem to have a few screws loose. Such errors of judgement can be dangerous.

Escaping from the soy paste vat

Editorial, *North American Daily News*
(New York), 24 August 1981

Bo Yang is one of the most popular writers in Taiwan today. His barbed, critical essays, belonging to a tradition of Chinese prose writing that developed after the fall of the imperial system early this century, are humorous, penetrating and provocative. The ten years Bo Yang spent in prison can be viewed as the consequence of being a social critic in China during a period of political transition. At the risk of causing displeasure to Bo Yang's loyal fans, we will discuss Bo Yang's essays from the historical point of view, placing them in the context of modern Chinese social criticism, and ignore his personal experiences.

The topic of Bo Yang's speech the other day was 'The Chinese People and the Soy Paste Vat'. The soy paste vat is not the only metaphor Bo Yang uses in his writings. But because he has used it in the past as a way of explaining some of the unhealthy tendencies in Chinese society, we will address it in our critique.

Bo Yang's soy paste vat is a wonderfully evocative metaphor. It is a common object of daily use, yet it provides an instant picture of all that is bad in Chinese society. In fact, Bo Yang performs the same basic function as every serious writer and thinker: he presents his readers with numerous ideas and lets them organise them in their own way. In this respect, few writers are as enlightening as Bo Yang. However, while Bo Yang's soy paste vat provides an effective metaphor for social phenomena, it fails to explain these phenomena. For example, if there was a correlation between the distribution of wealth in Chinese society on the one hand, and the contents of the soy paste vat on the other, we could use the distribution of wealth as a way of 'explaining' the social phenomena in the vat. Furthermore, we could attempt to use taxation and government financial planning to address those unhealthy

117

tendencies. Specifically, if a small number of people control the distribution of wealth (in the form of salaries) in an organisation, then that organisation is bound to be rife with favour-seeking and infighting. If we fail to perceive the relationship between the distribution of wealth on the one hand, and the phenomenon of favour-seeking on the other, then while people may be 'conscious' of the soy paste vat syndrome in general, this particular instance of soy paste vat behaviour is likely to be regarded as a problem related to the distribution of wealth, and thus not amenable to change. The distribution of wealth is just one example. The electoral process and the system of litigation can also serve as examples here.

There is no disputing Bo Yang's importance as a writer in contemporary China. He has made more Chinese people aware of their own deep-seated bad habits than hundreds of political scientists and sociologists with PhDs could ever do. But in reforming social behaviour, a distinction must be made between change in the realm of individual consciousness, and change in the realm of social consciousness, something that transcends the individual. By directing his barbs at the former, Bo Yang risks mockery and condemnation from all sides, but his contribution to the edification of the Chinese people exceeds that of any number of 'scholars' countless times.

We must sweep our faults under the rug and parade our virtues in order not to demean ourselves: some criticism and suggestions for Bo Yang

Xu Qin, *Huaqiao Daily* (New York), 11 September 1981

I read in the newspaper about Bo Yang's trip to the United States, and have great sympathy for him because of all the suffering he has endured. His visit to the United States is a major event for all those people who care about him. In fact many people had been hoping that Bo Yang would be able to shed some light on the crisis facing all Chinese people today. In his speech, which dealt with the question of the so-called 'culture of the soy paste vat', Bo Yang took 5000 years of Chinese culture, including the great civilisation created by the emperors of the Tang and Song, and in a single dismissive gesture flushed it all down the toilet. By so doing, Bo Yang makes us lose all our faith and pride in our culture. I trust Bo Yang's sincerity, and realise that what he says is based on his own unpleasant experiences. But considering his status in the Chinese community today, and the potential influence he has on people, Bo Yang has no right to set off fireworks in public without imposing some self-restraint. I feel I must make some constructive criticism of his soy paste vat theory. Bo Yang has not only destroyed Chinese people's sense of respect for themselves and their culture, but he has waved eunuchs and bound feet in front of foreigners' noses, giving them reason to make fun of us.

Objectively speaking, Bo Yang's viewpoint is that of an extremist. He errs in calling eunuchs and bound feet flaws in Chinese culture. Actually, they are nothing more than manifestations of sadistic sexual behaviour practised by decadent, self-indulgent dictators, and have nothing to do with true Chinese culture. To cite another example, some scholars believe that the rules of rhyme and metre in poetry set down in the Tang dynasty (618–907) are obstacles to poetic creation. Tang poets cherished vitality and naturalness. Their rhetorical rules were based on the spoken and written language of the time. Tang poems exhibit the true spirit of poetry—naturalness and creativity. Tang poets never expected later poets to follow the same rules they did. Such a view is simply pettiness on the part of post-Tang writers.

To give an example from everyday life, the Manchu *qipao* is a most graceful and elegant form of female dress, but the form-fitting *qipaos* women wear today with their side slits coming well above the knee are a far cry from the original design. It would be wrong to deny or ignore the fact that our ancestors kept eunuchs and bound their women's feet, but we all know that in traditional China people had a habit of 'concealing their faults and making public their merits'. In the history of the United States, the opening up of the Wild West is now regarded as an era of heroic exploration, the stuff romantic tales are made of, while the cruel, dark side of those exploitative decades is overlooked whenever possible.

All serious Western sinologists appreciate the beauty and subtlety of Chinese culture and many approach it with feelings of awe. The Japanese only began to imitate the West at the start of the Meiji Restoration in the late nineteenth century. But during the Edo (1600–1867) period and before, they drew upon Chinese culture to mould the very essence of their own civilisation. An eighteenth century Japanese painter who adopted a Chinese name, painted in the Chinese style and wrote Chinese poetry was praised as 'a true Chinese'! Today the streets of every Japanese city still bear visible traces of Chinese culture. While contemporary Japan is one of the world's most advanced societies, the Japanese people have never rejected Chinese culture, although they draw a line between themselves and the Chinese people, and deny there is a close blood relationship. No longer do the Japanese shout the imperialist slogan that was so familiar during the second world war: 'one culture, one race'. Maybe we Chinese people should ask ourselves how much of our own culture we truly understand, before asking what is wrong with it. Why must we demean our own extraordinary culture, and blame all the problems of China today on this specious theory of the soy paste vat?

China has a population of over 800 million people. The pressing issue in China today is how to unite so many people and bring happiness into their lives. Even the Chinese people who live in Taiwan would agree with this. In military terms, the Chinese people are capable of defending themselves, and most of them have the opportunity to receive an education. Neither Western culture nor Japanese culture can guide such a huge population towards modernisation, and at the same time give them a sense of spiritual identity. This task belongs to our own ancient traditional culture. Chinese culture is profoundly humanistic; it has a rich tradition of scientific thought; it has fine literature, art, handicrafts, architecture, music and costume in infinite varieties . . . Only Chinese culture itself can lead the 800 million Chinese down the path of civilisation and fill their lives with happiness. The Japanese people have drawn upon Chinese culture and have benefited from it greatly. Western people are studying it. As for us, the Chinese people, the last thing we should do is denigrate or disparage what is essentially ours. By doing so, we not only threaten the survival of the Chinese people, we also become the unworthy descendants of those who created this culture.

We cannot allow the Japanese people to make the claim that they are the rightful heirs of the Chinese cultural tradition. We should observe more, think more and judge more for ourselves. As Bo Yang said, we must develop our powers of judgement, not only to improve our own lives, but for the benefit of our 800 million compatriots.

The contemptible Chinaman

Wang Yiling, *Pai Hsing Semi-monthly*
(Hong Kong), 16 January 1985

I have just read Bo Yang's 'The Ugly Chinaman'. There is anger in my heart, and I must put it into words.

The Chinese people have suffered much over the past 100 years, and deserve our pity. In fact, their situation has only worsened over time. First came the Westernisation Movement in the nineteenth century, symbolised by Zhang Zhidong's famous slogan, 'Chinese traditional learning for foundation, Western learning for practical application'. An admirable concept, to be sure, whether or not it was practical, but at least it had a Chinese 'foundation'. But before long, the 'foundation' began to crumble. The next wave of reformers busied themselves cursing their parents for having endowed them with straight black hair and yellow skin, features that they could hardly wash or throw away; and while sighing and whining that 'the moon overseas is rounder than the moon in China', they blamed everything on their parents, grandparents, great-grandparents, etc. This was the essence of the May Fourth tradition, which dates back to 1919. At least the May Fourth boys were sensible. They only thought the moon in the West was rounder than the moon in China; they never went as far as praising foreign farts for their superior fragrance. The main reason for their attitude stems from the relative backwardness of transportation and communications in those days, when few Chinese had the means to ape foreigners in everything they did, unlike today, with our instantaneous worldwide communications. So when the Americans started calling themselves 'ugly Americans' and the Japanese 'ugly Japanese', the Chinese hopped on the bandwagon and in a flurry of books and articles the Ugly Chinaman was born.

None of the termagant progenitors of the May Fourth movement were of the common ilk. In fact all the May Fourthers who were shouting 'down with this' and 'down with that' in the name of progress were famous writers who regarded themselves as patriots. They wrote under assumed names, and one of them made a name for himself by producing three novels, *Home*, *Spring* and *Autumn*, in which he revealed his deep-seated hatred for traditional China. Unwittingly, perhaps, these patriots paved the way for Marxism and Leninism to paint China red: thus we can blame all the catastrophes of the past 40 years in China on those fashion-plate intellectuals of 70 years ago. And then Bo Yang appeared on the scene. Generally regarded as a fiercely patriotic writer, he has elevated the May Fourth spirit to new heights, first by ranting about 'the culture of the soy paste vat' and then by raving against 'the Ugly Chinaman'.

I am Chinese. I have many shortcomings and have made many mistakes in my life, some of them serious. But I am not an 'Ugly Chinaman', nor are all Chinese people 'Ugly Chinamen'. I don't know if Bo Yang is Chinese or not. If he is Chinese, he is free to call himself an Ugly Chinaman if he pleases, but he has no right to insult others in that way.

I disagree with the gist and tone of Bo Yang's 'The Ugly Chinaman', but I do not believe that the entire article is worthless. A few of the things he says are quite correct, such as:

> There is nothing inherently wrong with the Chinese people. I don't mean to be consoling: Chinese people are certainly not lacking in intelligence. Every university in the United States has Chinese students at the top of their class, and we have produced numerous noted scientists: Sun Kuan-han, the father of Chinese nuclear physics, and Nobel Prize winners C. N. Yang and C. T. Lee. There is no problem with our innate capacity, and I know we have the ability to make China a healthy and happy place to live. I also believe that China will some day become a great nation. But we must not spend all of our time and energy trying to make China a major military power. It is infinitely more important to bring some happiness into the people's lives. Once we achieve this, then we can concern ourselves with power and greatness.

I agree with all of this, especially the line about bringing happiness into people's lives. I am sorry that Bo Yang did not develop this theme further or make it the core of his essay. I strongly and absolutely disagree with Bo Yang's assertion that Chinese people are ugly.

After reading Bo Yang's article, one must ask what is really so ugly about the Chinese people? Bo Yang has a ready-made answer for this, of course, and he stacks up all sorts of odd evidence to prove that Chinese people are 'filthy, sloppy, noisy and always fighting among themselves'. I don't think Bo Yang is making this up, but even if he isn't, what is he trying accomplish? Is there any nation on earth where people are *not* noisy or contentious? Aren't American hippies filthy? Aren't the New York subways dirty and chaotic? Don't politicians in the USA, Europe and Japan hold shouting matches and play power games? And can you tell me they never engage in infighting? If you follow Bo Yang's logic, then the name of his essay ought to be changed to 'The Ugly Human Race'.

I find it inexplicably absurd that Bo Yang should make such a fuss about Chinese people's loud voices, and cite this as evidence for their 'ugliness'. I agree with the principle, 'When in Rome, do as the Romans do'. When Chinese people emigrate to the United States, as I did, they should try to change their Chinese habit of talking at the top of their voices, and to the best of their ability imitate the way cultivated Americans speak, that is, softly, and in a refined tone of voice, so that when they talk on the telephone, it sounds like a mosquito buzzing on the line. This is more important than you might think. But if a Chinese person has difficulty lowering his voice, this is not a serious crime. Is it really fair to call this 'ugly'? From this you can see how deeply Bo Yang hates the Chinese people. You can always find something nasty to say about other people, if you set out to do it.

Why does a well-known self-proclaimed patriotic author like Bo Yang bother to pile up so much half-baked, patchy evidence with the sole aim of depreciating his fellow countrymen? I have never met Bo Yang in person, but I once read an interview with Bo Yang written by a Ms Li Qi, who regards him as a great Chinese patriot, and says that Bo Yang has an ardent love for China and great hopes for the future of the country and its people. But when Bo Yang puts his aspirations into words, he ends up blaming everyone but himself, cursing and swearing as if it were going out of style. The basic reason behind this is Bo Yang's own perverse understanding of Chinese culture. It is quite possible that Bo Yang himself has unwittingly been misled by his own personal 'soy paste vat', and that his nervous system has been paralysed by 'germs' he has cultivated himself.

Chinese culture is vast, encompassing enlightened rulers and despots, benevolence and righteousness, whores and scoundrels, forthrightness and sincerity, effeteness and sentimentality. All of these things, both good and bad, have attained heights of unrivalled perfection in Chinese hands. Chinese culture is so exhaustive and comprehensive, that it should be easy to find in it a whole variety of 'soy paste vats' and a wide variety of 'germs'. In fact, it has all the chamber pots and bacteria anyone could ever want; all you have to do is look for them. If you want to declare that Chinese culture is a chamber pot full of bacteria, Chinese culture won't suffer in the least but it will prove that you are a hopeless stinking scum-bag.

Some of the great men who studied the Song-dynasty treatise, *A Comprehensive Mirror of Government*, learned to rule China in an enlightened manner. But when Mao Zedong read it, he refined his arsenal of techniques for torturing and brainwashing people, and eventually even outdid Stalin at his own game. Traditional Chinese culture is like a sharp knife. How you use it is what really counts. In the hands of a surgeon, a knife can save lives. In the hands of a murderer, it can kill people. And in the hands of a suicidal maniac . . . If anyone wants to go off the deep end and seek out soy paste vats and viruses in Chinese culture, then leave it up to an off-the-wall writer to do so. It's he who will end up catching the virus—not Chinese culture.

Here I would like to make a few irrelevant remarks. Over the past century, reactionary political movements in China have resulted in any number of scholars and literati being jailed, executed and arrested as political prisoners, a few examples of how the Chinese government pokes its head into every sphere of human activity. Because everyone loathes despotic governments, individuals who publicly defy authority can enjoy the sympathy and respect of the public, and in fact anyone who has been jailed for political reasons or victimised during a political campaign seems to sprout a halo around their heads.

I don't believe this is right, and it is also wrong to generalise. There are of course cases in which truly courageous people die in jail or are killed in the course of supporting good causes, such as those officials in ancient China who criticised the emperor at the risk of being chopped in half with a sword, or more specifically in more modern times, a group of journalists during the Republican period who risked their lives by exposing the corruption of the Soong and Kung families. Their incarceration and deaths had some significance and are worthy of our respect. But I see no reason to mourn the untimely deaths of such 'revolutionary martyrs' as Li Dazhao and He Yebin. And 'rightists' like yours truly only have ourselves to blame for our own fate. All 'martyrs' and 'rightists' in China were victims of political campaigns mounted by thoroughly vicious and tyrannical totalitarian governments. But the suffering that these people endured only caused harm to them, and brought no benefit to the people. In a word, anyone who suffers for nothing deserves to suffer.

Based on what I have suggested above, I feel that Bo Yang wastes his breath every time he opens his mouth and brags about the nine years and so many days he spent in prison—as if doing time in the clink was something prestigious like studying for an advanced degree abroad. If we follow Bo Yang's logic, then there's a writer in Taiwan today who's even greater than Bo Yang. After he got out of jail, he continued to write essays as nasty and biting as before he went to jail, and when he puts people down he curses their ancestors for at least 18 generations. What's the big fuss? At best this writer is just another hand-to-mouth Chinese intellectual on the run.

In sum, although Chinese people are not necessarily ugly, I know a few who are beneath contempt.

Non-sense of humour

Huixuan Chu, *Hong Kong Economic Journal* (Hong Kong), 23 January 1985

The current issue of *Pai Hsing* magazine has a rather polemical article entitled 'The Contemptible Chinaman' by Wang Yiling, which is a strong attack on Bo Yang. Wang starts out by saying, 'There is anger in my heart, and I must put it into words'. And indeed what he has written is a vitriolic tirade, without a hint of that gentle forthrightness and sincerity we associate with traditional Chinese literary exchanges. Wang doesn't refrain from using such blatantly uncouth language as 'stinking scum-bag' and 'beneath contempt', and even compares Bo Yang's stint in prison with going abroad to study. If we accept Bo Yang's premise in 'The Ugly Chinaman', then Wang Yiling is hoisting himself by his own petard. And while it may appear that Wang is contradicting Bo Yang, he is actually providing convincing evidence to bolster Bo Yang's argument.

Wang Yiling suffers from the same disability that has plagued Chinese people for thousands of years: the lack of a sense of humour. Could anyone imagine that Bo Yang is trying to write an academic thesis on Chinese ugliness in the hope of winning the Nobel Prize in anthropology? Social critics like Bo Yang write in order to stir up reactions in others and initiate debates, which is something quite different from compiling a research report based on hard facts. Obviously Wang Yiling disagrees with Bo Yang's point of view, but by losing his self-control he falls right into Bo Yang's trap. What is at issue here is not the question of whether Chinese people are ugly or not, but rather the way Wang seems to have become so enraged that he must have burned out countless brain cells.

The same issue of *Pai Hsing* magazine contains a letter from a Mr

Liang, who reacted to Bo Yang's 'The Ugly Chinaman' by becoming sad, then depressed and finally breaking down in a fit of tears! The way I see it, Liang's tears and Wang's wrath are like the pot calling the kettle black. Both gentlemen want to appear like Confucian moralists, who see the world in just, rational terms. This orientation prevents them from reading between the lines of Bo Yang's essays and enjoying the humour to be found there. Also, they can only come up with the weirdest, most misconstrued interpretations of Bo Yang's delightful examples and metaphors.

You cannot read Bo Yang without a sense of humour. He's a clown, a practical joker, waving the magic wand of wisdom before our eyes. It takes a certain open-mindedness to catch his gist. Ramrod moralists who take everything seriously are bound to miss his point.

Chinese civilisation has such a long history, could it possibly be free of flaws? When he picks at Chinese faults and weaknesses, Bo Yang is actually making fun of himself for the purpose of shocking us into doing a bit of introspection. Of course by focusing on the negative side of Chinese culture and leaving out the positive, he is only being modest. Anyone who thinks that Bo Yang is carrying out a painstaking autopsy on Chinese culture fails to appreciate Bo Yang's efforts. The last thing Bo Yang would want his readers to do is cry.

The Chinese people are a great people, both prettier and uglier than every other people on earth. It is certainly more constructive to depict the bad side of Chinese culture in all its ugliness, rather than sing the praises of its strong points. Put in another way, though the Chinese people are ugly, there is great beauty in their ugliness.

Ten manifestations of the slave mentality

Bo Ren, *Pai Hsing Semi-monthly*
(Hong Kong), 1 April 1985

Dear Bo Yang,

How have the Chinese people been able to tolerate despotic government for so many centuries? The answer lies in their slave mentality. In one of his more penetrating essays, Lu Xun wrote that Chinese history can be divided into two ages. One is called 'the age when the Chinese people wanted to be enslaved but couldn't', and the other 'the age when they were enslaved'. The Chinese people have never been able to think of themselves as the masters of China and hence have always acted like slaves. The message hidden in the soy paste vat tells them: China belongs to the emperor, the generals, the ministers, the heros and the warriors; the common people are destined to be slaves. Chinese people want to be slaves during prosperous and peaceful times; they happily pay their taxes and serve in the army when they are called up. This willingness grows out of the fact that over the course of Chinese history, such opportunities have been rather rare. If they are fortunate enough to live during a prosperous age, they will 'thank heaven' for their good fortune and do exactly as they are told.

The Chinese slave mentality manifests itself in ten ways:

1 Chinese people are addicted to shouting 'Long live So-and-so'. They have been shouting this sort of thing for so many thousands of years that it has become instinctual. The emperor of China is addressed as 'Ten thousand years' even if he is a bum, a thug or a common thief. As long as he's the emperor sitting in a palace, everyone will shout 'Long Live So-and-so' three times and kowtow to him. In the mid-twentieth century, this old custom underwent a novel yet hideous transformation. Even before the latest emperor made his triumphant entry into Beijing, people everywhere were shouting 'Long Live So-and-so'. Once he installed himself in Zhongnanhai, every time he appeared on Tiananmen Gate, cries of 'Long Live So-and-so' resounded up to the heavens; in fact people shouted so loudly their faces were covered with tears. I was one of those standing in Tiananmen Square. When I saw the Imperial Countenance, tears welled up in my eyes, and I shouted 'Long Live So-and-so' until I was hoarse. I shouted this every year, sometimes every day. In fact if I didn't shout it the sun would stop rising, and the earth would stop spinning.

2   Chinese people are superstitious by nature. They are innately superstitious about emperors. They elevate the emperor to heaven, while they themselves remain earthbound. They cannot see themselves as equals of the emperor, and actually believe that the emperor is a celestial immortal who has descended to earth, a living incarnation of the dragon. They feel the same way about modern-day emperors. Everyone knows the latest emperor started out as a librarian in a Beijing university, a common citizen of Beijing. But the moment he took up residence in Zhongnanhai, people treated him as if he were divine. They started worshipping him, developing superstitious beliefs about him, and made physical and mental sacrifices to him. People removed the image of the God of the Hearth from their homes and replaced it with his 'standard issue' portrait. This was taken to extremes during the Cultural Revolution when we had to sing psalms from the emperor's *Little Red Book* and perform the 'Dance of Loyalty'.

3   Chinese people respond uniformly to all tyrants, bullies and corrupt officials with a philosophy of resigned toleration. Whether it be press-ganging labourers, extorting excessive taxes, or mowing down innocent citizens, Chinese people respond in a uniform way: they tolerate, tolerate, tolerate. This tolerance reached unprecedented proportions during the reign of a certain modern emperor, when anyone who couldn't 'tolerate' was considered a scoundrel. How do you deal with brain-washing? Grin and bear it. How do you deal with being categorised as an unreformed bourgeois rightist? Grin and bear it. How about famine? Grin and bear it. And the same goes for all natural disasters, man-made holocausts, and the Cultural Revolution. Only he who can grin and bear it can make peace with himself—this is the traditional Chinese way, no Chinese needs to be taught it!

4   The Chinese people cannot appreciate authentic democracy, so they make a fuss about 'slave democracy'. In the Chinese version of majority rule, the majority are all slaves, so the minority has no choice but to be slaves too. Lu Xun wondered why, if monkeys can evolve

into human beings, there are still so many monkeys in the world? In fact, only a small minority of monkeys want to become human. Once upon a time this minority stood up on their hind legs and started walking around like people, and announced to the other monkeys that they had decided to become human. But none of the other monkeys would allow them to do this, claiming that this went against basic monkey nature, and started biting them until they bled to death. Not every single Chinese person wants to be a slave. There is a minority who want to be their own masters. But the other Chinese people refuse to allow this, and disclose the desires of this cantankerous minority to the authorities. Before long, this minority is arrested, thrown in jail and executed. This is how people become 'counter-revolutionaries' and 'rightists'.

5   Chinese people are cruel to their own kind, which perhaps explains their frequent infighting. When Chinese people are oppressed by tyrants and despots, rather than organising to fight the oppression, they start going for each other's throats. If the government accuses Mr A of being a 'crook' or a 'thug', then everyone will parrot the government and start calling Mr A a 'crook' or a 'thug', and help the government to round him up. This is quite common today, with the consequences for the victim turning out to be even more horrible than in the past. If the government launches a political movement that everyone knows will cause innumerable casualties, no one will dare to stand up and oppose it or raise their voice in protest. Rather they will start shouting the praises of the Exalted Leader's infinite wisdom, and throw themselves wholeheartedly into a fierce struggle against 'class enemies'. There is one problem, though. Some of these 'class enemies' that are supposed to be eradicated are either your friends, your relatives or your colleagues. So who do you eradicate first? And who wants to be arrested? Nobody's willing to volunteer. But this is an order from On High, and it must be obeyed. So there is a flurry of exposures, denunciations, criticism, and struggle sessions: you expose me, I'll inform on you; you criticise me, I'll denounce you. This gradually escalates until there is a further order from On High and a few unfortunates are picked up, handed over to the police, forced to attend political study sessions, have rightist 'caps' forced onto their heads, or are subjected to 'thought reform under the supervision of the proletariat'. And thus another political campaign comes to an end. And when the next campaign rolls around, the very same script is followed, and a fresh handful of 'class enemies' are cooked up in precisely the same fashion. In this snake-pit of mutual hatred, the winners are always the tyrants and despots.

6   Chinese people excel at acting shrewdly and playing it safe. What

does this mean? In mainland China, it means two things: first, never disobey orders from above; and second, in hard times, never show any sympathy for others. In other words, it means being a proper, diligent, obedient slave. The clever slave doesn't frame innocent people, but at the same time he doesn't protest when something is wrong.

Slaves are happy living with a false sense of security and muddling their way through life, no matter how low they have to stoop to accomplish this. For the sake of their own survival, if everyone else is beating a man when he's down, they'll do it too, and this act will be regarded as wise and virtuous. A former classmate of mine from China visited me in Hong Kong and said: 'If we had been together in the Anti-rightist Campaign in 1957, I would have turned you in'. In those days, this was regarded as wisdom. Tyrants and despots appreciate people who act like that, in other words, people with the slave mentality.

7 Chinese people survive on hope. They do not control their own destinies and allow their lives to be run by tyrants and despots, so they have never learned to use their own brains to improve things. Rather they embrace the hope that despotic rulers will magically transform themselves into enlightened sovereigns, and that tyrannical officials will turn themselves into upright upholders of the law, and make life easy for them. This is an old Chinese tradition, and few emperors have failed to take advantage of it and keep the people under their thumb. This holds true for today's emperors, who are still filling the Chinese people's ears with exquisite hopes: communism is heaven, they say.

When I was in middle school in 1949, I remember attending a lecture given by the philosopher Sun Dingguo. Professor Sun said, 'What is communism? It's drinking milk and eating bread!' In those days, our diet consisted entirely of steamed corn muffins and cabbage soup, so milk and bread sounded heavenly. Ten years later, there was still no milk or bread to eat, and we were still munching on corn muffins and washing them down with cabbage soup. But by then muffins and soup were rationed and we never got enough to fill our stomachs. Yet we still had our hopes—that steamed corn muffins and cabbage soup would no longer be rationed. But these hopes came to naught, and the situation grew worse. Finally, at the start of the Cultural Revolution, some people lost hope entirely and committed suicide. But this did not discourage the survivors enough to make them give up their 'philosophy of hope', and most people remained optimistic. This was only possible because they had no way to protest, and had forgotten that they were intelligent, individual human beings.

8 Chinese people are clinically and certifiably paranoid. Bo Yang hit the nail on the head with this one. Paranoia is an inherited Chinese characteristic. Chinese people have been suffering at the hands of tyrants for so long that they have grown accustomed to calamities falling on their heads at any time. And when the worst happens, it spells disaster not only for individuals, but for their entire family or clan. This sort of neurotic paranoia reached a peak in China in the 1950s. In 1957, a friend of mine was classified as a 'middle-class rightist', which was simply a warning that he had 'rightist tendencies', but had not crossed the line into the forbidden zone where he would have to wear a rightist 'cap'. But this made my friend so anxious that whenever an important Party document was read in study sessions, he panicked. By the time the Cultural Revolution rolled around, he was in such a state that when Mao announced his 'Sixteen Points', he was hospitalised for psychosis. Even today in China, countless people are suffering from this form of mental illness. Another friend from the mainland who visited me in Hong Kong said, 'You better be careful about what you write. 1997 [when China takes over Hong Kong] is only a few years away!'

9 Chinese people are bound by all sorts of odd conventions and restrictions, many of which are old, ingrained habits. As Bo Yang wrote, as far back as the Eastern Han dynasty, whenever scholars wrote essays, they had to confine their thinking to the contents of their teachers' essays. Overstepping these boundaries was a serious offence. Today these limits are even stricter, and apply not only to writing essays, talking to other people, and teaching in school, but also to marriage, death and even love affairs. What are the precise limits? The 'unassailable thought' of the Great Helmsman. Although these limits are rather abstract, woe to whoever exceeds them. Countless are the scholars, writers and artists who trespassed the boundaries of orthodoxy and wound up in serious trouble, or dead. Why do Chinese people love restrictions? Because. if they obey them, life is safe. Many people are so used to operating within a set of strict limits that it has become second nature to them, and they actually enjoy it! They never exceed the limits, so they don't allow others to do so either.

10 Chinese people are chameleons. In his story 'The Chameleon', Chekhov made fun of the Russian tendency to act like this remarkable creature. But Chinese people are also accomplished chameleons. Tyrannical rulers and corrupt officials love a good chameleon when they see one. This explains why the number of chameleons in mainland China has increased rapidly over the last 30 years, and why they can change colour with incredible speed. General Cao Cao of the Han dynasty has always been regarded as a villain. But along comes the

Great Helmsman with the claim that 'Calling Cao Cao a villain is unjust', so everyone revises their judgement. The First Emperor of the Qin dynasty has always been known as a tyrant. But when the Great Helmsman warned people, 'Don't be so hard on the First Emperor', everyone started to paint the First Emperor's portrait with a benevolent smile on his face. When the Great Helmsman appointed Lin Biao his second in command, everyone shouted 'Eternal health' to him. But when Lin Biao died in an airplane crash in Mongolia, the same people started to shout, 'Down with the crook Lin Biao!' Even more interesting is the way a petty party secretary gets treated like a minor deity, but the moment he is 'capped' as a capitalist roader, no one has any qualms about beating and kicking him at a mass 'struggle' session. And then when he is rehabilitated and becomes party secretary once again, people go back to revering him like a god, as if nothing had ever happened. Have you ever seen quicker chameleons?

For years, whenever people talked about what is wrong with the Chinese people, the blame was always laid on foreign imperialists. But the last 30 years have demonstrated that the blame lies with our own soy paste vat culture. In fact if the soy paste vat culture hadn't created a nation of Ugly Chinamen, the foreign imperialists would never have got their foot in the door in the first place.

The soy paste vat culture created despots and tyrants just as it created the slave mentality among the common folk. Tyranny and the slave mentality have caused untold catastrophes for China. And for the last 40 years, these two odd creatures have been strutting on the stage of Chinese history for one and all to see!

What is the solution? Here is where the real problem lies. I thoroughly agree with Bo Yang that the Chinese people must solve their own problems. But because we never look at ourselves in the mirror, we don't know how ugly we are.

Over the last few years, as China has begun to open its doors to the outside world, many young Chinese have had the opportunity to go abroad to study. They have been able to observe life in the West and make comparisons. Perhaps some of them have realised to what degree they themselves are Ugly Chinamen, and have made up their minds to improve themselves. Herein lies our hope. But is this another case of surviving on hope?

Culture sans civilisation?

Hu Juren, *Luntan bao* [*The Forum*]
(Los Angeles), 6 February 1985

The meaning of the terms 'civilisation' and 'culture' overlap in many ways. Everyone seems to have a different definition for them. There are even some chauvinistic Chinese intellectuals who claim that in the West there is no culture per se, only civilisation. Or they look down their noses and claim that America has no culture at all—although I have never heard anyone say that there is no such thing as American civilisation.

Let's turn this question around: China has a fabulous culture, but is it a civilised country?

Which is more important, culture or civilisation? Can you have culture without civilisation?

Actually culture and civilisation are inextricably linked, and mutually dependent. We can characterise the relationship between them by saying: civilisation is the embodiment of culture, and culture is the wet nurse of civilisation.

Civilisation comprises all the concrete manifestations of culture in society and daily life, the most obvious of which is etiquette. But when Confucius codified the 'rites' or *li*, he was dealing with culture. For 2000 years, the Confucian 'rites' found expression in the Chinese social system, including what people said and how they behaved, as well as in the various festivals, customs, rituals and ceremonies that took place during the year. This, in its entirety, is what we know as Chinese civilisation; in other words, civilisation is simply life.

If we accept this premise, then Chinese people are certainly a laughable lot. And since there is no such thing as Chinese civilisation any more, can we even speak of Chinese culture? When you get right down to it, Chinese civilisation (if there is such a thing) and Chinese culture are contradictory. So how can Chinese civilisation be the 'embodiment of Chinese culture'?

The point I wish to make is, the values that we cherish today do not belong to Chinese culture, but have been borrowed lock, stock and barrel from a foreign culture. Chinese civilisation is a bastard civilisation, only distantly related to its mother—traditional Chinese culture.

In *Step on his Tail*, Bo Yang describes how he discovered how polite Americans are. When I went to the US I got the same impression. In most social situations, Chinese people are 'primitive' and 'barbaric' compared to Americans, since we Chinese rarely say 'please' and 'thank you'. I am not exaggerating. If Chinese public behaviour can be taken as an expression of Chinese civilisation, it is certainly a far cry from that of the Americans, not to mention the Japanese or the Koreans.

What is the use of boasting about your ancestors' extinct culture if you don't behave in a civilised manner? Can you have culture without civilisation? You may think you have culture, but it's a bastard culture at best. And yet some insist on calling it Chinese!

Chinese culture shall not be besmirched!

Liu Qianmin, *Luntan bao* [*The Forum*]
(Los Angeles), 6 March 1985

Most people in Taiwan have heard of Bo Yang. Although I have never read any of his books, I have heard a lot about his trials and tribulations. Twenty years ago, when Taiwan was still a boring, provincial and rather repressive place, Bo Yang's social criticism was like a breath of fresh air, and he quickly made a name for himself. But quick and easy success has its attendant dangers. Bo Yang wrote about every subject under the sun, and thus it was inevitable that he would stray into forbidden territory, for which he won himself a free trip to the prison on Green Island. When he emerged from prison, his brain considerably enriched by ten years of meditation, he was greeted with instant fame. But as his fame—or notoriety—increased, he seemed to grow increasingly outspoken and contentious. He was one of a handful of writers at the time who, having tired of mere invective, took up the cudgel and started smashing, with a vengeance, everything past and present that appeared before them. Of course they didn't spare China's 5000 years of traditional culture.

I was deeply affected when I read the transcription of the speech Bo Yang gave in Iowa, 'The Ugly Chinaman'. It is true that if a country as vast as China continues to remain as poor and helpless as it is today, it may disintegrate once and for all. Today there are even university-educated Chinese living overseas who deny their Chineseness and want nothing to do with China for the rest of their lives.

Other Chinese people, noting the power and wealth enjoyed by people in the West, have adopted the slave mentality and claim that the moon in the West is rounder than the moon in China. And when they look in the mirror and notice how poor and weak they are, they

137

get frustrated and start bemoaning the worthlessness of Chinese people and Chinese culture. With the exception of people like Bo Yang and his ilk, I can think of no other examples in world history when the citizens of a poor country have displayed such outright sycophancy and resentment in their condemnation of their own countrymen and the very culture that they depend upon for a living. The Greek physicist Archimedes said, 'If you give me a fulcrum, I can pry open the earth'. Bo Yang probably dreamed about this fulcrum once—it appeared in his dreams in the form of the soy paste vat of Chinese culture—and he got the idea in his swelled head that he could use this fulcrum to attack and destroy China, with its population of one billion and its magnificent culture.

Books about 'national ugliness' have been published in two of the wealthiest societies in the world, the USA and Japan. Not long after the end of the second world war, an American wrote a novel called *The Ugly American*, and several years later there appeared a Japanese take off called *The Ugly Japanese*. Presumably the authors of both of these books felt that their fellow-countrymen had grown self-indulgent, immoral or just plain rude, and felt it was necessary to educate them about the reality of their own condition. In order to make his point, the author of *The Ugly Japanese* published the book while he was the ambassador of a Japanese mission overseas. As one might expect, he lost his foreign ministry job, but one never doubts that he had his country's best interests at heart.

I've been living in the United States for nearly 20 years. But as far as I can tell, most American people lead extremely busy lives, and it is hard to believe that something as insignificant as a book entitled *The Ugly American* would excite much interest among them. I imagine that few Americans have even heard of the book, not to mention read it. The situation in Taiwan is quite different. Even though the island is a beehive of industry and commerce, people manage to find enough time to enjoy leisure pursuits, and there has been no overall decrease in the traditional Chinese love of fun and excitement. If you don't believe me, walk down any street in Taipei's crowded Hsimenting district, stop for a moment and look up into the sky. I'll bet a heap that everyone nearby you will do the same. People in Taiwan are curious about everything. When Bo Yang published his *The Ugly Chinaman*, the book didn't exactly sell out on the first day it came out, but it did eventually become a best-seller.

When Chinese people get into arguments, they inevitably end up insulting their adversary's ancestors. The reason for this is simple: filial piety is an Achilles heel in Chinese culture. In his book, Bo Yang further refines the art of reviling by venting his spleen on Chinese culture. By applying the formula, 'the soil determines the quality of the fruit, the society determines the quality of the people', Bo Yang can condemn every Chinese person who ever lived.

The history of modern China is filled with endless incidents of domestic turmoil and foreign aggression, which have caused the Chinese people immeasurable suffering. Long periods of impoverishment and powerlessness have made Chinese people lose faith in themselves and their nation. There are now two Chinas: do we need to say more about the communist mainland than the fact that it is poor and backward? While life is better in Taiwan, with the average annual income now exceeding US$3000, it is still poor compared to the US or Japan. For this reason, I feel that at the present time, Chinese people should concern themselves with cultivating 'poverty without obsequiousness'; it will probably take another 50 years before we can start talking about 'wealth without arrogance' or 'wealth accompanied with good manners'. By then China may be ready for Bo Yang's 'The Ugly Chinaman'.

But Bo Yang is much too concerned with making a name—and a pile of money—for himself to be concerned with such things. He wants to ape the Japanese and the Americans and be the first Chinese person to hang all the dirty laundry in China on the line for the rest of the world to see. He's also ambitious, and doesn't want to go it alone. Bo Yang wants everybody to join in his vilification campaign and trample Chinese culture into the ground. Bo Yang learned a lesson from his bad experience in prison, and he knows that to accomplish anything on a large scale requires careful planning. So he tries to get everyone he knows to write about the Ugly Chinaman to publicise his own campaign. Of course this will also make it convenient for him if some day he needs to ask other people to bring him his meals in jail once again.

Let us now examine how Bo Yang's uglification campaign against Chinese culture has had a negative influence on the average Chinese. We will cite Bo Yang's own experiences as an example. Mr and Mrs Bo Yang's trip to Iowa was financed in part by Mr Fei Zhuzhang, the owner of a Chinese restaurant in Iowa. Bo Yang quotes Mr Fei as saying, 'Before reading your books, I felt that the Chinese people were a great people. After reading them my thinking changed entirely. Your books inspired me and made me want to hear you speak in person.'

Bo Yang added, 'When Mr Fei started thinking about the problems which exist within Chinese culture, he wondered whether there might be some basic defect in the moral fibre of the Chinese people.' Bo Yang's conclusion was, 'There is nothing inherently wrong with the Chinese national character. I am not saying this out of self-pity. Nor are Chinese people lacking in intelligence. Every university in the United States has Chinese students in the top of their class, and we have produced numerous noted scientists . . . The Chinese character is not fundamentally flawed . . . '

The 'character' Bo Yang is talking about has more to do with the Chinese people's physiology than with their cultural background. From the biological point of view, all human beings have the same brain capacity, measured in physical size, and scientists no longer believe that there are racial differences in this regard. Why do some nations produce outstanding accomplishments for a certain period in their history, and then enter into a period of decline? Why did England produce so many geniuses in Newton's day, while today the British as a people seem to have lost that spark of brilliance? Has the English-man's brain capacity shrunk since the time of Newton?

We all know that some blind people have extraordinary powers of hearing, even though their ears and auditory nerves are the same as those of sighted people. The key difference is the blind person's ability to make use of his organs of hearing. Chinese students excel in school and perform extraordinarily well on IQ tests. Sociologists, psychologists and educators have tried to figure out if this bears any relationship to Chinese culture. Chinese culture seems to possess enough tenacity, vigour and endurance to 'cure' whoever comes in contact with it of their laziness and stupidity: Japan and South Korea are just two examples of this phenomenon. Open the table of contents of any leading American scientific journal, and you will find that a striking percentage of the authors are Chinese. This clearly suggests that cultural back-ground is an important factor in intelligence. Whenever I am sur-rounded by the teeming masses of China, I get a feeling deep down that I am floating in a vast sea of wisdom and intelligence. Armed with his soy paste vat, it's not enough for Bo Yang to simply trample on Chinese culture. Yet he is unable to depreciate Chinese people's intel-ligence convincingly. The best he can do is to exclude intelligence from his blacklist of Chinese qualities. Here Bo Yang runs foul of logic, and exercises his 'judgement' before examining a question from more than one angle.

Bo Yang claims that China has made few contributions to civilisation, and that after Confucius, who died more than 2000 years ago, China produced not a single great thinker. According to Bo Yang, Chinese culture is a huge stagnant pond, which he refers to as a soy paste vat. As the contents of the vat ferment and exude ever more unpleasant odours, the Chinese people absorb them and start to stink themselves. This sort of logic is, to be polite, seriously lacking in common sense; or to put it more directly, Bo Yang is an intellectual hooligan. Every middle school student in China knows that Confucius was followed by such great thinkers as Mencius, Zhu Xi and Wang Yangming. We might say something about Mencius here. Confucius' political thought was expressed quite concretely and systematically in *The Book of Rites*. But his philosophical system was far from perfect, and its acceptance as the ideology of the State underwent considerable deliberation over the course of history. Confucius spoke of 'the gentleman' and 'the people', but he failed to elaborate satisfactorily on the relationship between them.

Mencius further developed the political thought of the School of Confucius. He said: 'If the gentleman prince commits serious errors, he should be criticised. If he commits the errors again and does not respond to criticism, he should be dethroned'; and 'The people are the most important factor in the country; the spirits of the land and grain come next; the sovereign is the least important'. In Mencius's view, then, the state and the rulers exist for the benefit of the people. If they fail to fulfil their appointed functions, they should, respectively, be dismantled, or dismissed and replaced. The basic spirit of Confucius's political philosophy can be summed up in one phrase: 'The world belongs to everyone'. Mencius elucidated the democratic tendencies in Confucian thought by emphasising that 'everyone' meant the people. Thus 'The world belongs to everyone' contains the seeds of two cardinal principles of democracy, 'government of the people' and 'government for the people'. For 2000 years, Chinese people spoke of Confucius and Mencius in the same breath. Actually Mencius was responsible for developing Confucius's thought.

The question of the negligible contribution China has made to civilisation must be examined from another point of view. The spread and dissemination of culture is entirely dependent on communications. In ancient times, all communications, both land and water, relied on human muscle power. For this reason, geography played a crucial role in the development and dissemination of culture in early times. (Have things changed much? Can land-locked Bhutan, tucked away in the Himalayas, develop into a commercial and industrial centre like Taiwan, Hong Kong or Singapore?) China's location in East Asia meant that it was cut off from the West by vast and nearly impenetrable deserts. These geographical obstacles had the effect of restricting the activities of Chinese people to the corner of the world they inhabited. For thousands of years, the Chinese people remained self-reliant and, lacking the conditions for interacting with the outside world, developed their own unique culture in their own solitary way. Western culture evolved in a totally different manner, with constant interaction taking place among numerous nations and peoples. Drawing on their combined wisdom, the Western nations were able to achieve breakthroughs in numerous fields, many of which have given the West its predominance in the world today. If there were no geographical barriers to inhibit cultural interflow between East and West in ancient times, or if China had been located in Europe, China would certainly have made numerous major contributions to world culture. For one thing, the 2000-year-old tradition of Confucian democracy would have had a significant influence on the emancipation of the slaves in ancient Greece and Rome. The First Emperor of the Qin dynasty's abolition of the system of feudal land ownership and the development of a political system wherein commoners could hold office would have had an edifying influence on the European Middle Ages that were slumbering along under feudalism. Finally, if China's great inventions, such as the art of printing, had been introduced into Europe 500 years earlier, the world would be a very different place today.

As we explained above, the main reason why Chinese culture developed to a high level and ceased to progress any further was China's geographical isolation, and thus it paid the price for going it alone. But the Chinese people can hardly be called cultural isolationists. In fact, of all the nations in the world, China probably has put up the least resistance to the influx of foreign thought and culture. The great changes that have taken place in China during the last hundred years have been dramatic: the sudden demise, only some 70 years ago, of the ancient imperial system, as a result of a single shot fired during the Wuchang Uprising; the fall from grace of Confucius, who after enjoying a position of eminence in Chinese civilisation for more than 2000 years, was shouted down over the course of a few days by young students during the May Fourth movement; the rapid spread of European-born Marxism, which became the 'school of practical learning' for intellectuals throughout China shortly after the May Fourth movement in 1919; the takeover of mainland China by the communists and the nationalists' flight to Taiwan, after the latter lost a civil war that had broken out at the end of the Anti-Japanese War; and finally, the announcement, after 34 years of communist rule, that China, now with a population of one billion, could no longer look to Marxism for the solution of all of its problems. Chinese people are remarkably gifted and flexibly minded people. The reason China is the way it is today is not because the Chinese people have rallied around the 'soy paste vat', but rather because they've been busy smashing it to bits. The Cultural Revolution is what happened when the Chinese people repudiated their traditional cultural values in a single stroke; they certainly learnt a bitter lesson from doing so.

Bo Yang thinks that filthiness and sloppiness characterise the Ugly

Chinaman, but that Chinese filth is slightly superior to Indian filth. I believe that the vast majority of Chinese people would disagree with Bo Yang's statement. In East Asia alone, the Japanese obsession with hygiene and cleanliness puts Japan on a par, in hygienic terms, with any other country in the world. Taiwan is a lot worse in this regard, but India is, well, the pits. When US President Jimmy Carter visited India, the TV news showed Carter at a state banquet with an Indian attendant standing behind him swatting a fly. In economic terms, Japan is rich, Taiwan is average, and India is poor. This suggests that a country's hygiene is directly related to its wealth. Los Angeles has two Chinatowns, one downtown [all inner cities tend to be filthy and chaotic BY] and the other in Monterrey Park. Monterrey Park's Chinatown maintains a high standard of cleanliness, while the downtown Chinatown is rather filthy. Both places are run by Chinese people. The difference lies in the educational background and family income of the local residents.

Chinese people often speak rather loudly when they are among other Chinese. Bo Yang picks on this unusual linguistic trait and sweeps it into the dustbin of Ugly Chinaman characteristics. He says: 'Why do Chinese people shout when they talk? Because we are insecure by nature. The louder we shout, the more right we are. If we shout at the top of our lungs, we must be right, otherwise why expend so much energy?' In one of his essays, Liang Shih-ch'iou suggested that Chinese people speak loudly because China has always been a predominantly agricultural society. When people go out into the fields in the morning, they shout greetings to each other, often from great distances. Some people believe that the way Chinese talk is related to the fact that Chinese is a tonal language. People in Suzhou, for instance, talk in sibilant whispers, and even when they argue they never raise their voices. I derive my own explanation of the high-volume phenomenon from several special characteristics of the Chinese language: each written character is pronounced separately; there are many homonyms; and, in standard Mandarin, each sound is pronounced in one of four tones. So if you don't speak loud enough, it is hard to be understood, especially if you are speaking quickly. These problems are especially apparent when watching Chinese movies. Without Chinese subtitles, it is often impossible to understand the dialogue.

The situation is further confused by Chinese grammar, which is also unique in the world. Unlike English, Chinese has no subjunctive case, and so Chinese people often have to use hand signals and perform extravagant vocal gymnastics in order to get their point across. If you are speaking softly and wish others to understand you, you have to speak slowly, drawing each syllable out as long as your breath permits.

I personally feel that trying to get Chinese people to lower their voices is a thankless and essentially hopeless task. If we accept this, we ought to enshrine our stentorian voices in the pantheon of essential Chinese characteristics, and take pleasure in our shouting!

Taiwan's chaotic traffic situation is pretty much a fact of life. But Bo Yang, to whom everything under the Chinese sun is grist for the Ugly Chinaman mill, attributes this problem to Chinese culture. As he put it:

> Since the many problems in this opaque, bottomless vat could not be solved by individuals exercising their own intelligence, the literati had to ape other people's thinking, or be led by other schools of thought. Place a fresh peach in a vat full of putrescent soy paste, and it will soon wither away and turn into a dry turd. China has its own unique way of transforming foreign things and ideas . . . You've got pedestrian crossing lines painted on the street; we do too, but they've been put there to make it easier for cars to run people over.

I've been concerned about traffic safety in Taiwan for many years, and here offer some ideas on the subject, if only to elicit further comments from those who share my concern. Traffic safety improves every year in Taiwan because the number of people who own private cars is on the rise. The sheer volume of vehicles on the road exerts a subtle pressure on everyone who drives to obey traffic laws. This is an example of the principle of 'live and learn'.

In the United States in addition to normal drivers there is a class of people known as 'defensive drivers'. Defensive drivers are normal drivers to begin with, but they have two special characteristics. First, they never exercise their priority rights, such as turning first at an intersection, even though the traffic laws allow them to do so; and second, if another driver does something offensive, defensive drivers are civilised enough not to seek revenge. Most drivers in Taiwan possess one or both of these characteristics, but the problem is that they do not qualify as 'normal' drivers in the first place. This has created the situation in Taiwan of 'order within chaos', and 'chaos within order'. Why are drivers in the US and China so different? We can get a clue from the way driver's licences are issued in these countries. In the USA, people learn to drive on the road, and thus are exposed to traffic laws and road safety from the moment they get behind the wheel. Driving tests are held on the road as well, and so drivers in America develop a good concept of what 'standard driving' is all about.

In Taiwan, people learn to drive in special training lots owned by driving schools, and are tested by the road authority for a limited number of skills on an electronically metered testing lot. The licence they are awarded if they pass the test would be more accurately called an 'operator's licence' rather than a 'driver's licence'. When they get on the road, Taiwan drivers lack standards for what constitutes correct driving, and thus tend to drive like savages without any regard for the rules. Even people who have been driving for ten or twenty years still make up the rules as they go along. I like to call this an 'elastic model', as it can be bent in any direction one pleases. In sum, Taiwan's traffic problems are not a human problem, or even a cultural problem, but rather a matter of government policy. Becuase the policy is flawed to begin with, the government can do very little to improve the situation.

This reminds me of an incident involving Alexander Solzhenitsyn, the Soviet Nobel laureate. Some time after he had arrived in the United States, he was invited to give a speech. Everyone was expecting him to make some profound remarks on freedom and human rights, but to everyone's surprise, he bashed the American economy. His specific target was American businessmen who sold food products that contained harmful preservatives with no regard for the consequences— except their own profits.

It wasn't long before the *New York Times* struck back. The *Times* said that while Solzhenitsyn had suffered in the Soviet Union for expressing his own beliefs, this did not give him licence to criticise American society in any way he pleased. And from then on, the US media stopped reporting any speeches Solzhenitsyn gave about the US food industry. Perhaps this incident frightened the Russian writer and he simply clammed up; or perhaps people stopped inviting him to speak any more. In a country where every citizen enjoys freedom of speech, neither the government nor the legal system can prevent people from blabbing about whatever they please or insulting people in public. But a powerful newspaper can act as a sheriff, and get the cops trailing you for the rest of your life. In China the newspapers aren't that powerful, but people respect public opinion. Let all Chinese people of good conscience stand up and say a few words of fairness on behalf of the Chinese people and Chinese culture.

Chinese culture: besmirch it or whitewash it

Zhang Xiaoqian, *Luntan bao* [*The Forum*]
(Los Angeles), 3–9 April 1985

The speech Bo Yang gave several months ago in Iowa on the subject of 'The Ugly Chinaman' made quite a stir among the Chinese living in the United States, and the excitement it caused has not yet died down. In a recent issue of this newspaper, I read Liu Qianmin's 'Chinese Culture Shall Not be Besmirched!', in which the author took Bo Yang to task for making disparaging remarks about Chinese culture, and for providing explanations for many of the faults and shortcomings of Chinese people.

Liu's lengthy article testifies to the fact that he has given much thought to the problems of Chinese culture. It is also clear from the article that Mr Liu loves Chinese culture deeply. I was most impressed with the spirit in which he conducted his investigations as well as his love for his subject, although there are many points on which I disagree with him.

1 Mr Liu urges Chinese people to accept 'poverty without obsequiousness' and put 'wealth without arrogance' on the back burner, as if this were unimportant today. In my humble opinion, these two attitudes are causally linked. For instance, if a rich and influential person is inordinately proud and arrogant and loves people to flatter him, then he will constantly be surrounded by professional bootlickers (*members of the tail-wagging brigade* BY). Only when rich and powerful people treat their friends with respect in spite of their poverty will their poor friends stop acting obsequiously.

2 Mr Liu said that England produced many geniuses in Newton's day, while today England has few geniuses to speak of. To judge whether England is really in decline, I turned to a list of Nobel Prize winners from

146

1960 to 1984, and discovered that in those 25 years, a total of 153 prizes were awarded in the sciences, 25.5 of which were won by Englishmen (the 0.5 went to an Austrian working in the UK), or exactly one sixth of the total, only second to the United States. After the first world war, England lost the pre-eminence in the sciences that it had enjoyed since the age of Newton, but it is an exaggeration to say that there is 'hardly a sign of life' in the field of scientific endeavour in that country.

3 Mr Liu said that the fact that Chinese people in early times confined their activities to one corner of Asia was deleterious to the development of Chinese culture. I find this point intriguing. Is this to suggest that before they colonised the New World, Europeans' activities were not confined to Europe? For example, in early times, both the population and land area of China exceeded that of Europe, and for at least half of its long history, China was under unified rule (beginning in the Middle Ages, Europe consisted of numerous nations separated by linguistic, cultural, political and religious differences), and there were obstacles to cultural exchange between different parts of the empire. Why then did the Renaissance, Enlightenment, the development of constitutional democracy and the Industrial Revolution all take place in Europe?

In my view, Chinese culture and technology ceased to develop in the Song dynasty because of the repressive influence of Neo-Confucianism. Even as early as the Han dynasty, state Confucianism raised many obstacles to the free exchange of scholarly thought. The Song Neo-Confucians, such as Cheng Yi and Zhu Xi, further narrowed the range of discourse, and believed that every individual, or at least every scholar, should devote all his energies to cultivating his individual self and becoming a sage. By the time Neo-Confucianism had become the mainstream of Confucian thought, much of the vitality of Chinese culture had been sapped. At the same time, the gentry bolstered their social status by arbitrarily creating four social classes—the gentry, farmers, artisans, and merchants—and relegated people with special skills—artisans and businessmen—to the lowest echelons. Technological breakthroughs were considered clever forms of trickery; they were likened to 'carving life-sized models of insects', and rarely received official support. In that anti-intellectual environment, the most talented people had little choice but to become officials, while the less talented drifted into the crafts and trades. In a society that disparaged scientific endeavour and commerce, how could there be any scientific progress? In the Southern Song dynasty, China had the necessary conditions for the emergence of capitalism. Had Chinese scholars enjoyed freedom of enquiry, and if the government had supported manufacturing and commerce, the Industrial Revolution might have taken place in China before it took place in England.

4 Mr Liu asks: 'Can land-locked Bhutan, far away in the Himalayas, develop industrially and commercially like Taiwan?' My answer to that is, where there's a will there's a way. For example, Switzerland is high in the Alps, with an even smaller land area than Bhutan. But Swiss industry is highly sophisticated, and Switzerland leads the world in several fields. According to Mr Liu's geopolitics, Spain, Italy, Greece and Egypt, with their excellent land and sea communications, should be the leading industrial and commercial nations of Europe. But they are actually poorer and more backward than land-locked, mountainous Switzerland, not to mention Norway and Sweden, which are tucked away in a far-away corner of the continent.

5 Mr Liu believes that the rapidity with which China has transformed its political system (for instance, from an empire to a republic) and economic policies suggests that the Chinese people are unable to resist the incursion of foreign ideas. One would like to ask Mr Liu if the aforementioned changes took place following a national referendum, or if they were approved by a democratically-elected parliament functioning according to parliamentary procedure? Mr Liu's argument makes sense only if the answer to this question is yes. But if these changes came about following a command from the top, or if they were sanctioned by a 'rubber stamp' legislature that exists only to serve the interests of those in power, then this suggests that Chinese people have no democratic rights. When the rulers of a country use guns to enforce their authority, they can choose any form of government or carry out any policies they please without worrying about whether the people approve or not.

Although the Cultural Revolution nominally set out to destroy traditional Chinese culture, the fact that it took place at all shows that traditional Chinese despotism is alive and well. It was also a wonderful display of vicious infighting. I believe that the Cultural Revolution is a pure, unadulterated product of the soy paste vat, and would never have taken place in a democratic country where there is respect for human rights.

6 Mr Liu claims that Chinese people speak loudly because the Chinese language is rich in homonyms, and so Chinese speakers must rely on shouting and hand signals to get their ideas across. If Mr Liu is correct in this regard, I hate to think how Chinese people communicate with each other on the telephone. You can't use hand signals when you talk on the phone, nor will shouting enable you to convey your message to the person on the other end of the line. I suggest that you ring someone up right now, and if you can make yourself understood without raising your voice, then we have to conclude that Mr Liu's argument doesn't hold water.

It is true that some Chinese people lack an understanding of parliamentary procedure and conference protocol, and will begin their refutation of another person's argument before he or she finishes speaking. This also happens quite often in normal social intercourse. Because everyone is trying to speak at the same time, you have to raise your voice in order to be heard.

7 Mr Liu wastes a lot of ink trying to explain that the reason why traffic in China is so chaotic is because Chinese people learn to drive on practice lots rather than on the road, as they do in the United States. Thus while Chinese people pass driving tests successfully, they treat public roads like a practice lot, and thus drive like irresponsible madmen. Though I know very little about driver education in Taiwan, it is easy to imagine that when people there learn to drive under controlled conditions, they have few opportunities to use their horns, and thus few opportunities to rudely prevent pedestrians from crossing the street at pedestrian crossings (otherwise they would have a hard time getting their licences). Why then, the moment they get out on the road, do they drive with their horns and ignore pedestrian crossings? I wish Mr Liu could explain this curious behaviour to me.

The above are some random thoughts that occurred to me after reading Mr Liu's article. Mr Liu said that Bo Yang is defaming Chinese culture. The way I see it, Mr Liu is whitewhashing some of the defects in Chinese culture. But whether we go out of our way to point out our culture's shortcomings, or attempt to whitewash them, I believe both authors have pure and honest motives. Thus Mr Liu's claim that Bo Yang is an outright xenophiliac is not only insincere but also unreasonable. If Bo Yang were really as obsequious as Mr Liu suspects, then Mr Bo would do well to lick the boots of the Kuomintang rather than foreigners' boots. A man of Bo Yang's gifts, given his background with the Save the Nation Corps (he was once the secretary general of the Young Writers Association of the Save the Nation Corps), could easily have secured himself a cosy little sinecure from the powers-that-be if he had been willing to mouth a few sweet nothings about the government in the right ears. But Bo Yang chose to make his living by speaking out against corruption, an enterprise that so inflamed the KMT that they locked him up for ten years. One can imagine a man of such convictions being somewhat proud in nature, but never obsequious. I wonder if Mr Liu would agree?

The wonderful Chinaman

Zhu Gui, *Pai Hsing Semi-Monthly* (Hong Kong), 16 May 1985

I disagree entirely with the conclusion Bo Yang makes in his speech 'The Ugly Chinaman', and offer in its stead an essay entitled 'The Wonderful Chinaman'.

In every Chinese community, the first thing you notice is that the place is 'crowded, noisy, filthy, and chaotic'. In my opinion, it's crowded because crowds make life exciting; it's noisy since Chinese people like things bold and brassy; it's filthy for the same reason that sunlight cannot be appreciated unless there is dust in the air; and it's chaotic because Chinese people are free spirits by nature.

Chinese people gather around the scene of an accident to show their sympathy for other people's suffering. This is why they love executions, corpses, fires, drownings and serious automobile accidents. The more harrowing the accident, the more eager they are to gawk. Missing out on an accident means giving up one of life's greatest pleasures! 'Pity the living, for their sufferings are many!' One of the great joys in life is to be able to stand on the sidelines and watch other people suffer, and to rejoice in the fact that it's not happening to you.

About fifteen years ago, when the super-highway linking the north and south of Taiwan was under construction, there was only one road between Taipei and Keelung. An accident occurred in front of the Hsi-chih Primary School in which a student was run over right in the middle of the road. The driver fled the scene immediately, and not a single one of the thousands of people who witnessed the accident would provide the authorities with a clue, such as the licence number of the guilty vehicle. Within minutes, a vast crowd had gathered around the scene of the accident, and despite the efforts of the police to restrain them, hundreds of curiosity seekers surrounded the tiny corpse and blocked the road. A man of about 40 could be heard shouting angrily, 'Motherf - - - er! They killed another one!' and forced his way through the crowd, as if nothing in the world was going to stop him from enjoying this once-in-a-lifetime spectacle. When he finally got to the centre of the action, his eager expression suddenly changed—it was as if he had been struck by lightning—and he broke out in a pathetic wail . . . Though this event took place nearly twenty years ago, when I close my eyes I see it again with striking clarity.

A few years ago, there was a huge traffic accident on the super-highway near San-yi involving some 60 or 70 vehicles. It started when one car ran off the road, but as other drivers slowed down and pulled over to enjoy the accident, the cars and trucks behind were unable to stop, resulting in one of the worst highway pile-ups in Taiwan's history.

In every Chinese community, tragic accidents are sure-fire crowd-pullers. If a house catches on fire, and the inhabitants are screaming for their lives trying to escape, you can always find a human wall of Chinese spectators standing between the fire and the firemen. If there is a mining accident, and hundreds of miners are trapped deep in the bowels of the earth, no matter how deep in the mountains the mine is, there will always be a trusty corps of 'concerned citizens' on the scene fighting it out with the rescue crew for a good viewing spot near the opening of the mine. No matter how inaccessible the sugar, the ants always find their way to it. There is nothing like a train derailment, airplane crash, flood, suicide attempt or execution to bring the Chinese ants out of the woodwork in droves.

Around twenty years ago, a man climbed up on the roof of a ten-storey building in downtown Taipei and declared he was going to jump. Within minutes the streets were crawling with curiosity seekers, who caused considerable difficulty for the police who were trying to spread out a safety net and send someone up to the roof to try and talk the man down. Journalists and photographers had their cameras aimed at the roof in anticipation of that precious moment when he would leap. But the man defied everyone's expectations, and despite repeated attempts by the police to dissuade him, he insisted that he was going to jump, and kept everyone waiting for two hours. When it comes to enjoying a good show, the Chinese are the most patient people in the world. That vast assemblage stood there for three entire hours craning their necks until they grew sore, and not a single person unglued their eyes from the roof. When the clock on the Taipei train station struck 11 am, the man still hadn't jumped, and not a single soul in the crowd had left. A housewife with a shopping basket over her arm who had witnessed the spectacle from the beginning could bear it no longer and mumbled to herself, 'If you're going to jump, man, get on with it, I've got to go shopping for lunch'.

Why do Chinese people love disasters? Because their own lives are one long disaster. Whoever has the misfortune of being born Chinese is destined to suffer most of his life. Calamity inevitably befalls every Chinese person, it's simply a matter of when and where. The Taoist classic *The Way and Its Power* has a passage that reads,

> Existence and non-existence give birth to each other; the difficult and the easy bring each other to fruition; the long and the short determine each other's form; the long and the short exist by virtue of their differences; pitches and sounds become harmonious by virtue of their interaction; what is in the front and what is in the rear follow each other.

This is to say that sorrow and joy, happiness and catastrophe are relative rather than absolute conditions.

He rides a horse, I ride a donkey. Looking ahead of me, I know I will never catch up to the horse. But behind me tere is a man pushing a cart. Though I am worse off than the man on horseback, I am way ahead of the man pushing the cart.

Others endure terrible agony, while nothing happens to me. Watching others suffer grievously while sailing through life is such a great pleasure that if you don't enjoy it to the full you are committing a sin of omission.

I recall one winter in Chongqing during the Anti-Japanese War, there was a ferry near the Chaotian Gate that you boarded by crossing a makeshift floating bridge when the river was low. The moment the ferry landed at the dock, all the passengers on board would perform that traditional Chinese acrobatic feat of attempting to pile onto the narrow gangway at one time in order to be able to disembark before everybody else. In the ensuing confusion that day, an elderly woman was pushed into the river. Hundreds of people on the ferry and lining the banks of the river watched her struggle for her life, and there were dozens of boats with people on them in the immediate vicinity, but no one made any attempt to help her. Then an American soldier in the crowd took off his overcoat, jumped into the river, and after a long struggle managed to haul her onto the shore. Having completed this heroic mission, he went back to retrieve his overcoat, but when he got to the place he had left it, it was gone.

Thirty-five years ago, I was involved in an accident at the Taichung train station in Taiwan that influenced me for the rest of my life. A stranger suddenly collapsed near the main entrance of the station. I wanted to help him, so I rushed about, found a bicycle rickshaw and took him to the hospital, but before I could complete the admission forms, he died. The hospital staff told to me to remove the corpse from the hospital immediately—they said its presence would spoil their business. Here I was, recently arrived in Taichung, with a strange corpse to dispose of. What was I to do? Fortunately the hospital called the police, who naturally asked me a series of questions about the identity of the deceased and the cause of death, and then told me to find a place to keep the corpse until the coroner could examine it and file his report.

I spent the next day trying to locate someone related to the dead man. When a person came forward, the first thing he asked me was, 'Where is the $50 he had on him the day he died?' After this, the police hauled me into the station and told me to give them a formal statement, write a report and provide them with a guarantor, all of which took me a month. Finally, the dead man's relative came forth and confessed that he had made up the story about the missing $50 because he was afraid I would ask him for the money I had spent hiring the bicycle rickshaw and paying the hospital fee. He almost had me there, but fortunately he was a basically honest peasant. Had he claimed his dead relative had $50 000 on him the day he died, I would still be in jail today.

Chinese people show their sympathy for others by unabashedly enjoying themselves while other people are undergoing devastating pain and anguish. Similarly, when others are successful or have something to celebrate, Chinese people respond with covert, hostile envy. The broadminded, magnanimous Ugly Chinaman cannot tolerate someone he knows doing better than himself, especially if the two of them have endured hardships together, and the other manages to break away. An old, colourful expression is apt here: 'Begrudge a poor man the layer of skin that forms on his gruel'. Two people can only afford to eat rice gruel. One of them happens upon a little extra rice, so he adds it to his gruel, which thickens to the point where a skin forms on the surface. The other despises him for this extravagance, and never lets him live it down.

Two people are perfectly content eating plain noodles. There's no strife, no friction. But then things change, and one of them enjoys a bowl of noodles with shredded pork. Then the other has the nerve to eat his noodles with juicy spareribs. How can they forgive each other? 'I'm starving, and you're starving too', so no-one feels hungry. 'I'm drowning, and you're drowning too', so no-one feels as if they are drowning. If you want to kill yourself by jumping down a well, it's much more comfortable if someone jumps down the well first to give you a soft cushion to land on. In Chinese society, people who end up as failures will always point to a successful person who owes them a debt of gratitude. In China, never take a job with a successful friend. Likewise, successful people should never hire old friends to work for them.

Chinese people have never practised hero-worship. In fact, Chinese people only worship pathetic failures! Guan Di, the god of war, only became an object of worship after he lost his kingdom; the Tyrant of Chu only became a hero when he committed *hara kiri* on the banks of the Wu River; and Zhuge Liang was only revered as a great strategist after years of loyal service in the court of Liu Bei. If Guan Di had taken Jingzhou, if the Tyrant of Chu had become emperor, and if Zhuge Liang had revived the Han dynasty, it is unlikely they would have been treated with such respect by later generations of Chinese. For similar reasons, Chinese people have a deep reverence for the dead, and hardly any reverence for the living. If someone with a family background and education similar to your own gets ahead of you, can you afford to stand aside with your hands behind your back? Vindictiveness is one of those outstanding Chinese traits that have been jewels in the crown of our culture for thousands of years.

The Chinese people have always been fastidious about making peace with powerful foreign nations, and have always invited the fiercest barbarians to ride roughshod over them, never taking offence when they pissed and shat on their heads—even welcomed such treatment with open arms. But if one celestial should rub another the wrong way by causing a slight irritation or making a mild complaint, the latter will do everything in his power to trip up the provocateur, such as attack him when he isn't looking, lay traps for him, or knife him in the back. Even worse, he'll display that talent for which the Chinese have been famous worldwide since ancient times—informing on their friends. Indeed Chinese people are geniuses when it comes to snitching. No matter what political system they are living under, those who hold the power of life and death over others inevitably develop a keen passion for informing on others, and blindly follow up every nasty rumour that brushes past their ears with the ravenousness of a dope fiend craving a fix. Way back in the Qin dynasty (221–207 BC), the prime minister Shang Yang passed a law to punish people who were guilty of false incrimination, but the Chinese people, always reluctant to discard anything from their illustrious past, seem to have let this law fall by the wayside.

My old friend Zhang is a talented calligrapher, painter and seal carver, a perfect gentleman of the old school who is always frank and outspoken. During the Northern Warlords period (around 1920), someone accused him of being a member of the Revolutionary Party, and he was sentenced to death; but before the sentence was carried out the Northern Expedition stamped out the Northern Warlords. During the Manchukuo period (in the 1930s), he was accused of being a 'Chonqing partisan', and was again sentenced to death; but the Japanese surrendered one day before his scheduled execution, otherwise he would have surely been a goner. When the communists occupied Manchuria in the 1940s, he was arrested as a 'traitor' and a 'KMT spy', and was sentenced to death for the third time. Later, in an exchange of prisoners, he was taken to Taiwan, where he was accused of being a 'communist spy', and sentenced to seven years imprisonment. Zhang is 82 years old now. One wonders what he'll be accused of next . . .

As individuals, Chinese people are unquestionably clever and intelligent. When they work hard, they are unbeatable. But oddly enough, ruling the Chinese nation of a billion souls is as easy as herding sheep. Chinese people can endure more hardships and swallow more humiliation than any other nationality on earth. If there were some sort of Olympics to determine who could tolerate more blame, suffer more insults, and swallow more contempt from others, the Chinese would make a clean sweep of the gold medals. Besides, they excel at lining up by the million (like worker ants) and being whipped into submission to complete huge engineering projects like the Great Wall of China or the Grand Canal. A warning: don't bother trying to improve the lives of the Chinese people. The smartest way of dealing with them is to listen patiently to their complaints and show them a little sympathy; that's all they really need in life.

In China, people are always willing to 'break the pot to make sure that no one has anything to eat'. But no one thinks it's worthwhile to 'gather firewood to build a communal fire'.

In Chinese films, whenever there's a tragic scene of a starving or homeless widow and her children, there isn't a single dry eye in the audience and the theatre resounds with sobbing. It is as if the life story of everyone in the theatre is miraculously being shown on the screen. Only in cinemas can Chinese people let their feelings of sympathy for others find full expression—'I'm starving, and you're starving too; I'm drowning, and you're drowning too'. But when the film ends and the audience leaves—still sniffling, mind you—and there's a crippled child or a sick old man begging on the pavement outside the theatre, and the 'concerned citizens' of China walk right past them with their noses in the air. This is because Chinese people live in two worlds, and have split personalities. One world is the ideal world, where everyone is kind, considerate, filial, benevolent and charitable; the other is the real world, full of war, starvation, suffering and death, a dog-eat-dog world in which all the virtues of the sage emperors Tang, Yao, Wu and Shun can't buy you a crust of bread. The *Book of Odes* and the *Analects* of Confucius can't be fried in a wok or steamed in a pot. Putting the world in order is other people's business. All I know is when my belly starts to rumble.

China is an ancient country with 5000 years of history and 5000 years of suffering. The great ancient sages bequeathed us a corpus of theories on how to run our lives, but 5000 years of confrontation with bitter reality have left us with a corpus of tried and tested methods which have enabled us to survive. Theoretical treatises tell us how to act under normal conditions, but reality forces us to act in an entirely different way. The 'ideal' and the 'actual' world are contradictory, but as neither of them can be ignored, it is necessary to live in both worlds simultaneously, and to cultivate a separate personality for each of them. In the ideal world, Chinese people are moral, loyal, loving, trustworthy, peace-loving, etc. In the real world, Chinese people are struggling on the edge of starvation, poised treacherously on the brink between life and death, with survival as the primary concern. You cheat me, I screw you. There's nothing I won't stoop to as long as I continue to survive. In the ideal world, good advice on how to behave is only given for other people's benefit. In the real world, people only act for their own benefit. This situation makes it impossible to learn what a Chinese person's true intentions are by listening to what he says. If he says he hates standing on ceremony, you would do well never to be casual with him. If he says he doesn't feel like saying anything today, you had better get him to start talking. But it's not so simple! People mean the opposite of what they say, right? Wrong. Chinese people say the opposite of what they mean sometimes, and what they really mean at other times. Even if you had the privilege of being a tapeworm in someone's belly, you would never have the foggiest notion of what he really thinks.

Zhang and Wang are old friends. Zhang's son is about to get married, but Zhang doesn't invite Wang to the wedding. This provides Wang with some potent ammunition. Let's eavesdrop as Wang attacks Zhang after the wedding:

> **Wang**   You don't think I'm good enough for you, eh? Your son gets married and you don't even tell me about it.
> **Zhang**   They're just kids, I didn't want you to go to all that trouble for something so trivial.
> **Wang**   What sort of rubbish is that? I thought we were good friends. You don't even send me a wedding announcement!
> **Zhang**   I'm terribly sorry, really I am. My younger son is getting married on Sunday. I'll make sure I send you an invitation this time.

Wang Huh?

Wang then tells everybody he meets that Zhang is using his sons' weddings as a way of showing off his wealth. And he even informs the Bureau of Personnel Administration that Zhang has broken one of the regulations stipulated in the 'Ten Reforms for Public School Teachers'.

The classical Chinese philosophers were overly optimistic, held idealised views of human potential, and made too many harsh demands on people. They set standards of behaviour impossible to attain, both then or now. If anyone were to attempt to live their lives according to their standards, they would immediately become a laughing-stock and would likely burn themselves out in the process. The sages also harped on the notion that 'If you can't be a sage, it's better to be a beast'. Actually only the clay and wooden images in Buddhist and Taoist temples can attain immortality, and while significant differences separate animals and men, people are human after all! Although people have immortal tendencies, they don't start out life as immortals. Although people have animal tendencies, they are different from animals to begin with. There is an old saying: 'People have six emotions and seven desires'. The critical goal in life is survival. Several thousand years of suffering have made the Chinese people extremely shrewd and clever. What is their highest principle? What is their greatest ideal? Staying alive. Chinese people would like everyone to be public-spirited, to show consideration for the weak and aid the disabled, to approach the problems of the world as if they were their own problems, to come to the aid of those in distress, and to act in a just and fair manner. But a few thousand years of practical experience have taught the Chinese people to mind their own business. In Chinese society, not minding one's own business can cause an infinite amount of trouble, and even lead to death. The best way to survive in this world is to be like a turtle, which pulls its head back into its shell whenever the situation calls for it. There are several popular Chinese expressions: 'Shovel the snow in front of your own door, don't bother with the frost on your neighbour's roof'. 'Take good care of yourself; don't worry about others.'

Here is another object lesson: a man riding a motorcycle had been struck by a car in the middle of an intersection in downtown Taipei. He was lying in a pool of blood in the middle of the road, and looked as if he might be dead. The car that had hit him had fled, and all the cars that streamed by swerved to avoid him; of course no one stopped to help. And then a taxi driver came along and, apparently moved by the victim's plight, bundled him up, took him to the hospital, paid the deposit for the treatment, and left feeling satisfied that he had saved a human life. When the man recovered, he started imagining that the taxi driver who had saved him was actually the culprit who had run him over, and took him to court. When presenting his case, the injured man stated that no complete stranger would go out of his way to take a bloody near-corpse to the hospital and pay for the treatment *unless* he were the one who had run him over. The judge accepted this testimony and charged the good-samaritan taxi driver with manslaughter. Because of his 'stupidity', the taxi driver had to sell his taxi to pay the victim compensation, and also spent six months in jail.

One sultry, rainy day, a bus I was on was packed to bursting, and all the windows were closed, making it nearly impossible to breathe. A young hooligan got on the bus and lit a cigarette, and within seconds everyone's eyes were smarting and noses were running. But not a single person on the bus would tell him to stop smoking. In China, if someone violates the rights of two or more people, none of those victimised will raise a finger in protest. The victims say to themselves: 'I am not the only sufferer here. If other people can put up with it, why should I stick my head out and offend someone?' If there were an Olympics for patience and forbearance, the Chinese would take all the gold medals.

If a Chinese person's rights are infringed upon and if he discovers that others are in the same situation, he will always submit to the humiliation, retreat from the confrontation, and never be foolish enough to cause offence when this could result in helping others without benefit to himself. When other people's rights are violated, Chinese people play the role of the 'concerned' bystander. Why would anyone who wants to keep his hands clean mess around with dog shit? You call such people heartless? If they weren't heartless they wouldn't live to the age of 100.

Being born Chinese spells disaster. For 5000 years the Chinese people have struggled on the brink of starvation and strolled back and forth in front of the gates of hell: 'Having enough to wear and eat takes precedence over concerns of glory or shame; only when the granaries are full can attention be paid to rituals and etiquette'. When your life hangs by a thread, there is little time left for gratitude and politeness. If you haven't had a bite to eat for four or five days and have dark circles around your eyes, you can't afford to be fussy about avoiding dog meat or beef; you wouldn't think twice about eating human flesh if your life depended on it.

An ancient Chinese sage said: 'Inequality is more distressing than scarcity; insecurity is more distressing than poverty'. This is one of the most inane statements ever made. How can you worry about equality in a time of 'scarcity'? If you have to divide up an apple among 10 000 people, how do you ensure that everyone gets a piece? If you're living in 'poverty', how can you possibly be at ease? If a man hasn't eaten for a week, can you expect him to be courteous to others, and then retreat quietly into a corner and die? 'Inequality is more distressing than scarcity' teaches people to accept hunger and suffering as if they were the norm. 'Insecurity is more distressing than poverty' teaches people to march obediently from the brink of starvation towards the valley of death. Not all rich people are generous, but poverty and stinginess are conceived in the same womb, and are a natural breeding ground for 'selfishness'.

I cannot judge whether all Chinese people are selfish, but I recall one incident that took place back in 1949 that sheds some light on the subject. A man who worked in a state-run factory had a hole in one of his shoes and needed a piece of scrap leather to fix it. He discovered that the ten-metre-long leather belt that ran all of the machinery in the factory was made of just the sort of material he needed, so he sneaked into the factory one night and cut a piece about 30 centimetres long from the belt. As a result, the factory had to shut down for two months, since in those days belts like that had to be imported from abroad. Considering that the man was poorly educated, and his shoe was falling apart, one can perhaps sympathise with him. But one expects university professors to be better educated! A group of professors were visiting an institution that was famed for its fine garden. The pride of the garden was a huge wisteria plant that was growing on top of a pavilion. The plant had a single stalk that climbed up the side of the pavilion and spread out on the roof like an umbrella. One of the members of the delegation thought he might take a cutting of this magnificent plant home with him, and when no one was looking, he took a pair of shears and cut himself a section of the stalk. Chinese people never think twice about causing harm to others if they can benefit from it in some way.

A single dyke can protect the lives and property of hundreds of thousands of people. But in order to earn a few pennies, a Chinese person would snip off a piece of wire connected to the floodgate, and sell it as scrap metal. And if there is a flood, with thousands of people drowned and billions of dollars of damage, the response is, 'That's their problem, it has nothing to do with me'. This is precisely what happened in the flood of August 1959.

You may also recall how several years ago, a consignment of veterinary penicillin was auctioned off to a businessman who repackaged it and sold it for human use. People were dying like flies, but the culprit was never prosecuted. We still hear of clinics in Taiwan selling used plastic syringes. Or when the government buys a huge piece of equipment, worth over ten million US dollars, and someone saws off a steel rod to use as a cane, even though it's only worth a few bucks, he can claim it now belongs to him. If you can't understand this, you aren't a true Chinese.

We should be grateful to the authorities for having installed automatic doors in all public places in Taiwan, as this greatly reduces opportunities for Chinese people to lose face. Back in the days of spring doors, the Chinese way was to kick a door open and barge in without looking to see if anyone was coming, which resulted in many an innocent person getting their nose flattened for no good reason.

People in Taiwan have plenty of money, and the tourism industry is well developed. The buffet restaurants now popular in tourist spots provide Chinese people with a wonderful opportunity to demonstrate the superiority of their traditional culture. Chinese people love to say things like 'being taken advantage of is a blessing', but no Chinese alive wants to be taken advantage of. At a buffet lunch, they will pile up their plate with enough food to kill an elephant without considering whether they can finish it or not. And then out of modesty they will make a point of eating less than the other people at their table.

'The earth is home to all creatures and things.' Chinese people treat China like a hotel, a place they might stay in for a few nights, but never for long. The Chinese always go for quick profits and short-term benefits; petty utilitarianism runs their lives. 'Officials don't build their own offices' means that one should never do anything that someone else might benefit from. 'Young people don't plant walnut trees' because it takes fifteen or twenty years for such trees to bear fruit. In ancient China, most buildings were made of wood and earth, even though more durable materials such as bricks and tile, iron and stone were available. Chinese history goes back thousands of years, but most Chinese buildings are only a few hundred years old.

The Chinese people have little regard for the earthly hotel they occupy, and minimal consideration for the guests who will stay in it once they check out. This is because with their history of living on the verge of starvation, they may keel over and die at any time and any place, which leaves them little leisure to think about anything else but survival. The Chinese attitude towards vital natural resources can be summed up in three old adages: 'Kill the chickens for their eggs', and 'Stop up a stream and catch all the fish'; rarely are they farsighted enough to 'Raise sheep in order to clip the wool'. Wherever the Chinese live, they overwork the soil, rape the forests, eat all the birds and animals, overfish the seas and lakes, and in general exploit the earth until it turns into a desert. In once-thriving Yongzhou, 'there is water but no boats, and nine out of ten mountains are barren'. One reason why Manchuria (Northeast China) and Taiwan are relatively rich today is because they were settled later than other parts of China.

'The gentleman who is fond of wealth must accumulate it morally' is a sensible old saying, and of course there is nothing wrong with acting morally or wanting to get rich. Wealth and morality are not mutually exclusive. But throughout history Chinese sages have harped on the fact that they are contradictory. 'Conduct your friendships properly, but do not seek profit from them; make your morality manifest, but seek no benefits from doing so.' This old saw simply encourages hypocrisy by encouraging people to be righteous and ignore profits, and to shy away from success in any form. You can sermonise in this manner all day, but the real world doesn't work this way at all.

Every Chinese educated in this century was taught to think about the Boxer Rebellion in the same way: 'The gradual spread of Western utilitarianism in China had a demoralising effect on the Chinese people'. Actually, the opposite is true. No-one in the world is more pragmatic than the Chinese. Before doing anything, the first question is, 'Is this going to do me any good?' Before Newton discovered gravity, turds dropped straight into the latrine. After Newton had discovered gravity, turds continued to fall straight into the latrine. Before he made his discovery, not a single turd flew up to the sky. The Chinese will never produce an idiot like Newton. As far as Chinese people are concerned, Galileo's discovery of the law of falling objects was a waste of time and energy. Since this law has no practical value, sages should ignore it.

Chinese people worship any god that can bless them with a winning lottery ticket. If they win the lottery, they go through the motions of thanking the god. If they lose, then they curse the god for being a hunk of clay. Chinese believe in anything that can bring them benefits, and are wary of anything that can bring them no benefit. Pragmatism has discouraged Chinese people from developing religious fanaticism, from producing martyrs and from fighting religious wars.

Chinese history records few love affairs in which both parties die for their love. Chinese people are taught the Middle Way, the way of moderation, and from birth are urged to keep their emotions in check. This actually boils down to pragmatism. Chinese never get overly enthusiastic about anything, and are reluctant to take a firm stand on any issue. What matters most is the bottom line. Everything is weighed carefully to determine whether it is 'worth it' or not.

When something bad happens to a Chinese, the first response is, 'What's the use?' Someone victimises you or entraps you; your wife and children leave you; you want to get your revenge and set things straight, because you have been wronged. But your friends will tell you, 'What's the use? Sure you've been wronged and want to get back at them, but you can't revive the dead, and your wife's gone forever, so why bother?' 'What's the use?' and 'Why bother?' are the two little questions that explain why China will never have a just society, and why Chinese people cannot act according to principle.

For similar reasons, Chinese people never take great risks. Chinese believe that only fools do dangerous things in their crazier moments. 'A son worth a thousand ounces of gold will not sit under a building with a crumbling roof.' 'A wild tiger may cross the river and die without regrets. But I would not do such a thing.' 'Real' Chinese think that only idiots go parachuting, take a boat over a waterfall or ride a motorcycle through a wall of fire, since they only provide some momentary thrills and have no practical benefit.

When Chinese people attend conferences, they never express their own opinions, and once the conference is over, they will still keep their opinions to themselves. It's a waste of time having a serious discussion with a Chinese. If suggestions are being solicited, no Chinese will open his mouth. Once the issue has been resolved, however, Chinese will immediately offer their own ideas on the subject. Chinese never agree with others on an issue, nor submit to any rules or regulations, so wherever Chinese people congregate there is bound to be chaos. Chinese show no consideration for other people's feelings, nor care what happens to them. When Chinese talk, they expect the whole world to listen to them. They talk loud enough to make the roof shake in order to overwhelm their interlocutor before he has a chance to open his mouth. Two Chinese people in the same room are as loud as 200.

Chinese communities are always filthy. There are more than a billion Chinese people in the world; can they *not* be crowded? In addition to being noisy, crowded, dirty and chaotic, they also love to watch others suffer and only plough the snow that accumulates in front of their own door . . . They love to talk about 'righteousness and humanity' while acting in a selfish and greedy manner. They tell you, 'Be kind to people and animals', while at the same time they will be fighting among themselves.

The Chinese people are a great people; in fact, they are so great it is hard to understand how they have survived for 5000 years!